It's

# Faith
# Family
# Fitness

## By Jeremiah Clark

It's all about Faith, Family, Fitness ©
Copyright@2017, Jeremiah Clark
Contact Jeremiah Clark at:
jc79miah@gmail.com

Names, characters, places and incidents are products of the author's imagination or are used fictitiously. Any resemblance to actual events or locales or persons, living or dead is entirely coincidental.

Published in the United States of America by Createspace.
First edition paperback printed January 2017.
All rights reserved.

ISBN-13 978-1539329046
ISBN-10 1539329046

# Disclaimer

I cannot be held responsible for any attempts of trying the exercises I mentioned, or changing your eating patterns to the ones mentioned in this book. I am not licensed in any way to make informed decisions about your health and fitness. I am only sharing my experiences and opinions about fitness and nutrition from my point of view.

Please consult your physician before trying anything mentioned in this book. Everybody has different backgrounds and limitations to consider before trying new exercises or new diets.

# Dedication

I want to dedicate this book to all who struggle with finding a purpose in life, and also to those who struggle with their health. I know life is hard, but I also know it can be a beautiful life despite that. My prayer has always been to help people in some way to lead them through life. I hope this book will help in some way.

Thanks everyone and remember,

Be Strong and Be Kind

Jeremiah

# Acknowledgements

I would definitely not be at this place in my life physically, mentally, or spiritually without the help of many people both past and present. There have been those who have left either a positive or negative impact on me. No matter which one was left on me, I needed them both, because each person has been helpful and vital for me to help shape my character.

First, I want to thank my wife, Stephanie, for being by my side all these years. People don't have to stay with each other. They can do whatever they want, and she chooses to stay with me every day. I'm beyond grateful for it. She has been vital in helping me become the man I am today in all areas of my life, and I'm so honored for her love toward me.

On a lighter note, thanks for taking the cover photo, Stephanie. Who knew there would be deer poop exactly where you would need to be sitting, and lying on the grass capturing the right angle? You were cold, tired, and wearing poop covered pants, but it shows the love you have for me, and I'm grateful.

To my kids Katie, Hannah, and Austin, all of you have been my inspiration for this book. I love you so much, and I will always try to lead you honorably in this world as best I can, so you can lead this world honorably with Jesus as your inspiration.

I want to thank all my close family and friends. I have needed so much help in all areas of my life at one point or another, and you have been there to step in and save the day. I will not forget those who sacrificed their time, energy and resources to me and my family.

I want to share my appreciation to all the pastors and church members who have influenced me from all the churches I have visited over the years, and for all the spiritual guidance and inspiration.

My mom and brother who continually watch over me and guide me in any support I need. Despite our difficult relationship over the years, I still want to thank my dad for introducing me to exercising and the fitness world that I have been lucky enough to enjoy all these years.

I thank the Five Star Life program (fivestarlife.org) for changing my perception on life, and showing me through serving and sacrificing that helping others is the path to real happiness. I'm so inspired by the leaders there past and present.

A big thanks to Tom Russell, a long-time friend. I used to deliver product to his brother's business several years ago, but we were able to re-connect several years later when we both coached for Five Star Life.

His experiences there with that awesome program led him to write two novels. He is the person who has inspired me to write my first book, because he never let circumstances deter him from following his dreams. Watching what he did gave me the courage to write this book. I asked for his involvement in this project, and he excitedly accepted. The year-long calls and text messages helped to keep me on track. The final process of launching this book would not have happened without his support and expertise. I would definitely check out his two books on Amazon to read also. They both have great positive messages in them, and that is what we need in the world.

"Finding Your True North: A Bullied Teen's Journey of Hope."

"Nowhere Man."

# Introduction

You don't usually hear about success stories about teenage couples who beat the odds of teenage pregnancy and have a successful, happy marriage and family life.

What about if I add that during my marriage, only one believed in God? According to most marriage and couple statistics, we should have went our separate ways years ago.

Along with being married several years, we have been blessed with three incredible children who are following our dedicated path of faith.

Coupled with that, we have focused on our fitness to help lead us to a strong physical, mental and spiritual life.

I must admit, however, this did not happen overnight. It took years of personal turmoil, but once I connected the dots, it ignited a passion in me I never saw coming.

I hope you are not being misled here. All this has not come easy. I have come so close to losing my marriage, kids, job and even my faith more than once, because of my stubbornness and ego.

I intend for this book to be a positive tool to use as a reference to what not to do, to stop doing the same things I was doing.

My favorite quotes incorporated throughout this book give a glimpse of how much my life has been impacted by other people's influence. I have read so many over the last few years, and I could easily inundate the pages full of them. The ones on these pages have helped me to reflect and evaluate my thoughts at different stages throughout of my life.

My faith story has been an incredibly meandering journey. To me, I was clueless as to God's great power and grace; He was with me all along.

As a teenager, and even through my early adult years, I had no use for God. The evil that I witnessed in the world on a daily basis, coupled with cogent explanations from science books took away any curiosity I had.

Years later, after really digging deep in research about how evil can change people's perspectives, and relying on science books to discredit God's existence, it ironically led me to become a Christian.

Once I became a Christian, I saw a transformation in myself whenever I visited churches. I discovered I had innate leadership skills that enabled me to propel me to a bigger passion in my faith journey. People told me I had a unique way of spreading my message that they can relate to with my excitement and unwavering faith.

I let them know my limited knowledge of the Bible was my Achilles heel. Yet my strength was how I led the youth groups, which gave me confidence to speak about my faith and fitness story to anyone who would listen.

I saw people start to see this connection and knew that I had to get my point of view across somehow. I have used social media and personal conversations to spread the word, but I believe this book will lay out all my important thoughts on the three topics.

So here it goes: a former atheist turned Christian, a workout fanatic through high school and my demanding job at Coca-Cola, and a dedicated family man who made crucial mistakes in the beginning of my marriage, will show how to throw Faith, Family and Fitness together for a more complete life.

If you disagree with my opinions, I'm fine with that. I have learned from experience that no matter what I believe, someone will not think the same way somewhere. I have learned after all the judging, name calling, cussing, and bullying I have shamefully done over the years, that people all want the same thing--at the end of all the arguments and difference of opinions, people want to be loved, respected and honored.

Sometimes we are just going about it the wrong way. So if you disagree, I respect that. On the parts you disagree, I just hope you can brush it off and find another part of the book that might be helpful. Again, I'm so honored you have decided to spend your time reading this book…Let's do this.

**"The quickest way to fail today is to promise yourself that you'll do it tomorrow." -unknown**

People all over the world are asking themselves, "Should I pursue my goals today, or should I throw it on tomorrow's to-do list and hope for the best?"

I'm actually a pretty logical-thinking person so I know that everyone must get up and commit themselves to their work, school, and family commitments daily.

I do the same, and that is very important to get done, or at least close to it every day.

Did you notice that word in that question above? Should? There is a way to find a balance on acting on the logical stuff and also going for the "your potential" stuff that needs to be applied when making decisions.

What else besides the logical stuff am I capable of taking on today? The answer to that question will depend on so many factors from your personal life's experience. Is this a crazy thought to consistently want to improve what I am capable of doing every day? It sounds like a lot of stress and hard work to be thinking so much about every day.

Why should I care what my limits are for the day? Why should I care what you are capable of every day?

Years ago if you were to ask me about my goals or what I think about your goals, I would have said, "I really could care less." Now, asking me that same question today I totally would have a different and more positive response.

I wish the whole world would think less like the first response. That is the purpose of this book. While I know that I'm just one person, if I'm able to help one person from the information I present in this book, I'm satisfied. I'm sticking with the whole Mother Teresa quote:

**"If you can't feed a hundred people, just feed one." - Mother Teresa**

I've come to a point in my life where I wanted to put my thoughts in print for a few reasons: the first is I always liked the concept of leaving notes, letters, pictures for my family and friends to be able to have as keepsakes.

A few years ago I came across a brand new Father's Journal at a garage sale. I consistently filled it up with as much of my personal feelings as I could.

Then a few years later I saw a college professor on TV giving a very powerful lecture on how to make a positive mark in the world. He was diagnosed with terminal cancer, so he felt it was imperative to reach out. The video eventually went viral, prompting Oprah Winfrey to invite him on her show.

His lecture turned into a book, titled, "The Last Lecture" by Randy Pausch. He originally intended to speak his message to only his three boys, but he had a bigger effect on the world.

A year ago, my friend Tom Russell wrote a book, "Finding Your True North: A Bullied Teen's Journey of Hope," based on his experiences with a group of middle schoolers who were in an after school program called Five Star Life. He wanted to impart a message of empowerment for those kids who have felt the indignities of being bullied by exposing the main character to these five core values: sacrifice, integrity, respect, responsibility and courage. This book has impacted me, but more importantly, hundreds of people who have read his book have been impacted as well.

I also had a lot of personal experiences from the same program with the kids, so I felt I also had a message or idea to share with the world. That program was a big part of my life. The combination of those events mentioned above gave me enough courage to write this book.

So, now I have been inspired, and have the courage to write something. But the difficult thing is I have never thought of myself as an author. What I do for a living is deliver product. What I did with this book was totally getting out of my comfort zone. If that isn't courage, I don't know what is.

I wish I could have the idea of writing about a boy wizard who goes to wizard school, but that idea was already taken. Thanks a lot, J.K. Rowling.

I decided that even though millions of people have degrees, and may be better qualified to write amazing books on similar topics, I know now that I bring to the table my own uniqueness to this idea of faith, family, and fitness; all three need to be present to have a balanced life.

I have been told by enough people and now see how those three things put together has paid off in my life. This is not the "mission accomplished" phase of my life, though. There is another mission now:

**"It's not about how good you are; it's about how good you want to be."-Paul Arden**

I want to pass along my experiences in life to help people succeed. I don't want to see myself or others have to see what happens in their life if they leave things status quo:

**"If you don't make the time to work on creating the life you want, you're eventually going to be forced to spend a lot of time dealing with a life you don't want." -Kevin Ngo**

So what do you say? Let's start this book and start making choices to keep fighting the good fight because:

**"The same voice that says "give up" can also be trained to say "keep going."-unknown**

# Faith

## Chapter One

## A Field Trip To Remember

I love the fall season. That may seem like an odd and random statement to tell you, but fall weather is something I can't wait to experience every year. I couldn't live in a place that doesn't go through it every year. Fortunately, I live in Indiana, which has beautiful fall weather.

I remember as a kid always looking at the beautiful array of colors on the trees, and just soaking up all the fall time activities that go along with it, one of them visiting pumpkin farms.

It was no surprise, then, when I was excited to learn that I was going to the yearly kindergarten field trip to a pumpkin farm, and enjoying all the fun stuff they offered for the students every year. I remember my mom signing me up and going along as a chaperone. That was a bonus, because my mom worked a lot, and I would get to spend time with her at the pumpkin farm.

What I didn't know was that I was going to experience something life changing that I have never forgotten.

I'm well into the third decade of my life, so to remember something so distinctly when I was five years old is very impactful. My mother was in another area of the farm, while I left my friends at the gift shop. I headed down the road a short distance to the entrance of the farm.

It truly was an amazing fall day. The weather was typically cool, overcast, with leaves blowing everywhere from the cool breeze.

As I was walking down the road soaking it all in, I stopped suddenly in the middle of my tracks and surveyed my surroundings. As a naïve kindergartener, I still could appreciate the beauty I was seeing. The trees were swaying in the wind, allowing a peaceful solitude I had never experienced before as a youngster. I had such an overwhelming love for life. A voice popped in my head, "This is an amazing world; you're going to have a great life."

I don't know if it was my naiveté or something pulled me out of the glorious trance, but the feeling soon disappeared. What's really sad is that feeling has never resurfaced to this day. This quote has reminded me of the trees I have randomly looked at all the time, but this time:

**"It's not what you look at that matters, it's what you see." -Henry David Thoreau**

You see, I wasn't just looking at my surroundings at the moment. I saw beyond the moment. Years later, I actually revisited the same area, but it didn't have the same effect on me as that time.

In fact, when I went there, I was so frustrated about the "Is there a God" question. I was looking for answers, and thought it would be a good place to go to get them, seeing how I had some kind of moment there I couldn't explain. Unfortunately, I didn't get any.

I didn't know God then. I was so young, and my mind probably was going a mile a minute. Random thoughts were rifling through my brain. The most prevalent one was how did I remember what I was feeling that day so clearly?

This thought really frustrated me, because no matter how much I wanted to shrug it off, I would argue that I knew there was someone or something up above. But you couldn't convince me there was a God. Today, I simply can't fathom I could even think that.

It's important for you to understand that now when I get upset with the world for how it is, or my faith is shaken because of my human nature emotions, it's no surprise that God chose my favorite season to get my attention. I always become more spiritual during the fall season. I just love it. I am so grateful for God and Jesus, and what they stand for.

# Chapter Two

## He Has the Whole Word
## In His Hands

The title of chapter two is a real song sung to many young children in Sunday School over the years. As an adult some still believe this, while others think it's full of you know what.

Well, let's talk about that, shall we?

It's important for me to tell you about my experience, because I believe many of you have had moments of your life when you were traveling and reveling in the beauty of this planet.

There is a powerful connection between us and nature. My struggle with faith had a lot to do with seeing such beauty in the world, but at the same time being taught through years of schooling that nothing but random chance created this universe and planet Earth.

Yes, I'm going to talk about this topic, and I hope you respect my honest conversation about it. I personally believe you must take on this elephant-in-the-room question of "Did God create the universe?" Let me be clear with you, if you are expecting me to have all the answers, I'm not a theologian. My goal is to help someone who is probably reading this and struggling with the same questions that I once had.

This book is not going to be a lecture all about this topic, but I do think I need to share a few points, the main one being we weren't around to see everything from the very beginning. It simply amazes me that brilliant scholars insist they have all the answers, though they can't seem to have total empirical evidence of the beginning of our existence.

After talking about this, we still will have questions that can't be explained, no matter how much evidence we come up with to either disprove or prove to people God is behind it.

My advice to the ones struggling with this question is to go to the library and research the Bible, and any book associated with showing God's involvement with creating this universe.

With further research, I also made it a point to peruse books that are purposely trying to discredit God, and show they have the answers for all of life's mysteries.

Why am I asking for you to do that? Because while I do believe God is behind it, I still had questions. You will be taught by many teachers one way or the other, depending on what type of school you go to.

Politics are now heavily involved now in making you choose one side or the other, and picking a political party based on a few ideas.

There are some churches with hidden agendas, and some let their agendas out in plain sight. There seems to be more time spent preaching, talking, and debating about politics than the Bible's true intention.

There are some scientists who let politics influence the results of their studies or research. When politics and money are involved (and they are and always will be) you need to be cautious, and do your own research.

It's the safest way to get answers, and that way you can be at peace with yourself that you were not brain-washed or misled into your way of thinking. You should know enough by the end of your researching this sensitive topic how you believe and, most important, be at peace with it. It's definitely a question you must figure out at least enough to be at peace to move forward. I want to share some of the points of my research on both sides of the arguments.

It starts with the science part of my faith, because I believe that is the key process to this whole thing.

After reading my thoughts, many people will question my loyalty to God, because I have lots of questions. I seem to have thoughts that don't coincide with the very strict teachings of some churches about science and interpretation of the Bible.

I was always frustrated by the churches that seem to dwell on debating others, even picketing social stances, and displaying a distorted view of the Jesus I knew. If a church concentrates on you having to believe on exactly the same political parties, taking a strict view on how God made the world, and are steadfast on their views and values, be careful.

They will say they are doing God's work by defending His values, but I'm pretty sure that He is more interested in them showing love and grace to others rather than arguing your points that results in shoeing them away.

No one comes to Christ by insulting them. So let's start with the science stuff. While we are at it, let's continue on with all the different complexities of faith that divide Christians into groups, and make others distance themselves more from the church because of their actions

Let's get it out of the way so we can move on to show that once you have your faith figured out, we can show how it all ties together. Sound like a plan? Good.

# Chapter Three

## Let Nature Take Its Course

I always like that saying. When a crazy moment happens in your life, sometimes that's a good way of dealing with it.

Basically, it's saying "Let's just see what happens." These situations happen a lot in life, but is this a view we should take with how we are here now on Earth? Let's look at a few ideas of how people are trying to figure out life's complex mysteries:

The Big Bang Theory-- Did God start it, or did a random chemical collision set it off? In any case, what did the universe explode into? From another universe? Complicated stuff here, isn't it? Moses, the author of the book of Genesis, gives credit to God creating it.

Now God's truth is in the Bible's words, but just as a story being told to many people, everyone hears it differently, even though the story is the same.

In my opinion, the Bible is vague on details on this topic. I'm sure that's for a reason. Even though I would love to have straight forward answers from Him, I trust my God on his process of explaining it.

Science has stumbled across a way he may have done it. I personally have no problem with their theory on this. Some objects out there look very random on how they are flying around out there.

At the same time, there seems to be some plan out there in a randomly growing universe out there. The size of the universe is really so big and powerful we will never fully understand the size. I'm sure there could easily be more life out there; the odds are definitely more in favor than not.

Evolution-- The word basically means changes over time. First of all, I can see with my own eyes looking around the world that plants and animals change and adapt according to where they live, what they eat, and how to protect themselves. Any of those factors could or have changed over time, and everything changes to survive better.

This world is coming close to convincing itself that using all the scientific research and then calling it evolution is how they are using method to discredit God, and what the Bible says about the creation of life.

I use to think that I now know God created it. You can call it whatever you want, but the word is just a summary of how science and research has evolved over time.

Now the first rule in science is observe. They were not there in the beginning of Earth being made, so they use the next best way to figure it out. Nothing can be 100% accurate because we were not there to see it happen.

How old is Earth? I have no idea. Some say 10,000 years old, because of how they figure out the family generations of the Bible. I don't remember God telling us to find a math puzzle in the Bible to figure out the age of Earth and the Universe.

I don't know why Creationists are so dead set on this idea? Is it billions and billions of years old? Maybe the billions sounds more realistic to me, but I really don't know. I really don't dwell on this. Actually, is it really that important?

We have more important issues to discuss than something that neither side can truly prove. Let's focus on solving world problems than debating one another from Creation Science people and scientists who seem to have a huge grudge and passion to argue about this stuff. It has less to do with God, and more about a political game to them.

Life begins on Earth--Oh no, the ape question. Hang on, first thing first. I am always fascinated with one question about how there was supposedly no life on Earth. Just rocks and gases, right?

We are to believe that a one-cell organism just popped into existence, and from there started the Evolution process that eventually led to us. How can something come from nothing?

This is a great thought, because not even the ape idea could be true with that theory, because a one-celled organism can't just pop into existence from thin air. Without the existence of that organism, we couldn't have the apes later on, and so on from there.

Dinosaurs--Creationists say that dinosaurs and humans were living during the same time frame, and were even on the Ark. Well, I wasn't there, but if you think about it, many dinosaurs were carnivores. Not many of the animals would have survived.

I believe Creationists mean well, but they have been politically motivated, and are influenced by money to promote an idea or political party no matter what to defend the Bible.

God created beautiful giants years ago, and have no problem with them being separated from human existence. I do have a problem with T Rex and little Johnny running around playing with each other just because for some reason Creationists have the need to combine these two, so it somehow fits into the Bible?

There is nothing that I saw in the Bible that tells me this needs to happen in that way to make it align with God's plan.

I trust God of His creation of the giants, and don't need a book or verse on them to convince me. I'm perfectly fine accepting the curiosity, and the discoveries of them as they show themselves through their fossils on Earth.

Oceans-- I have always been confused on this. I know that God made them, but even from a scientific view, how did all that water get on a planet that didn't look like it does now? The planet is covered with water. It truly depends on the oceans to maintain life, and the tides just happen to be controlled by the moon, which is conveniently there to help out with that.

The weather systems of the world not only depend on the oceans, but even on the Himalayan Mountains located in Asia north of India. The elevation height of the mountain range is at a height that enables warm air from the India region to come north into the mountains, and start cloud formations that are responsible for the weather around the world. Crazy, huh?

There are so many other examples of life connecting together to work, but we need to move on to more topics.

Apes R Us--Pretty strong evidence, right? If you didn't know about God, and someone gave you all the results of the research of the apes, and told you they found out how we were created, would you believe them?

That is what happened to me. Some things that stood out to me were the similarities of our bodies, and the fossils found around the world. The DNA evidence of 98% match is also a strong case, and to me the aggressive way they act and treat other apes are so similar to the greediness and hate that humans show one other every day in the world presently.

People also have seen the caveman drawings in caves. It is mostly universally accepted that they exist. Even believers who claim they don't believe in the evolution theory, they need to understand that cavemen are evolved apes. For the longest time I believed that until I looked at it from a different perspective.

I present a random Harry Potter quote for this thought. In a particular scene, Harry tells Dumbledore that he has been having these thoughts lately, and he believes his thoughts were just like the Evil Voldemort, Dumbledore tells Harry Potter:

**"Harry, it isn't how you are alike, it's how you are not."**
**-Dumbledore**

Back to this issue: God's love is not ascribed to what the world thinks is love. I've seen so many qualities of love displayed from one human being to another in the world. Love happens despite the evilness that reigns here. I truly believe no amount of evolving could make humans behave that way for reasons to survive better.

I've heard reasons being kind to each other makes the world a better place. Well, it certainly makes sense to treat each other that way, so that we could be better than we were back then, but I truly don't believe it would make sense to treat people with love in a survival-of-the-fittest world.

The logical way to survive is to behave aggressively toward self-preservation. We see this behavior in animals all the time, and, unfortunately, in people as well. Coincidence? Maybe.

When it comes down to it, I honestly don't have a concrete answer. What I do know is God made us. It seems like a good way to expand life, to let things happen and change accordingly on Earth and with life.

I could provide some empirical evidence again, but honestly, it's how I feel inside. I have researched both sides of the argument for years now, but my faith has not been shaken. Oddly enough, even as a Christian, I still had questions.

I have talked to science teachers who teach evolution, and who also believe in God. I have also talked to pastors who are at peace with the topic, knowing both sides still pursue God passionately.

My advice would be to research people who do amazing things in God's name. That behavior is not normal in this cruel world. Look for stories of scientists becoming believers in God, and also believers leaving the faith because of science. Study both sides to get your answers, because I know only you can know deep inside what the truth is. The world will always be divided on this, so it's up to you decide which side you're on.

My advice is too also pray about it. Yes, I know some of you would never stoop so low to do such a thing, but if we are going to be as real and open minded as we can, pray to God and get real with him. I know He values sincerity.

Ask for your curiosity to be answered about life's mysteries, and maybe even question His power. Ask him to show His power, grace and love to you. I remember praying many times these very thoughts. The more authentic my conversation was with Him, the more He showed me his power. It never ceases to amaze me.

I'm ready to move on to another area. How about you? Good luck with your journey with those topics if you are currently searching, or are about to dig into it. I will end with this verse in the Bible that helped me immensely. God is basically saying "check out my creation. It's there for you to see and learn from. Its ever-changing beauty is there for you."

*"The heavens declare the glory of God; the skies proclaim the work of his hands. Day after day they pour speech; night after night they display knowledge. There is no speech or language where his voice is not heard. His voice goes out into all of the earth; his words to the ends of the world--*
*Psalm 19*

# Chapter Four

## "It's up to you to find beauty in the ugliest of days"- unknown

This will be a hard chapter to write about, because I struggle with many topics discussed in this one. I'm talking like every day.

Sure, we just took on the science world, and figured that not only did I struggle with the realities of what we are about to talk about, but I know that many others have the same thoughts every day.

Now, just because we have these thoughts, it doesn't discredit our faith. It simply makes us stronger and pushes our faith to heights that could never be reached, unless we struggled with it every day

I believe we need to talk about evilness of the world. Who is behind it? Why everyone, especially Christians, are frankly losing the battle because of their double standards on how they are living their lives, instead of making this world a far more beautiful place to live.

A lot of bad things happen that have understandable consequences, like all the chemicals we have been putting in our bodies either by eating the food that for decades have all kinds of questionable long term effects, and the chemicals that we deal with like cleaning supplies. Sometimes certain jobs deal with extreme types of pollution. Even the medicine we take for good reasons have questionable long term effects that may even be passed down to each generation.

Bad habits and addictions are other unfortunate causes of it too. A lot of those problems are directly created by bad habits that should have been avoided.

Now, we need to discuss the unexplainable and pure evil acts. That's where I and others have had doubts at some point in our lives. Why does evil exist? If God is greater than evil, then why does he allow evil to reign supreme? Does this sound like I have given up on God? I hope not, because my faith in God has overcome all this, despite its realities and the results of evil doing its thing around the world.

I believe we need to go back to the beginning of the story that was told in the Bible, where the birth of evil occurred to have some understanding of evil and the power of it. I say some, because it has been made clear in the Bible that we are dealing with powers far greater than what we think is going on, just like the universe. We are never going to fully understand the vastness and determination to overpower God and the influence of evil.

The quick version is God created an angel almost parallel to him in beauty and power. This angel, named Lucifer, (Satan or Devil) deceitfully recruited angels fighting for his cause, and battled God and his angels. They lost the battle and were thrown down to Earth, banished from heaven forever. Unfortunately, Satan and his followers are still around presently with only one agenda: to destroy us. He wants to keep us away from God in every way possible.

I kept this story short because you can read so many books about evil. I am not a pastor, who could tell this story of the Bible so much better. This battle that happened long ago is very serious. And while I believe that it was an event that we cannot even fathom, we need to wrap our heads around this to clearly understand why the world is the way it is.

There is a battle consistently 24/7 going on between God (light) and evil (darkness) for you and the way you live on Earth and beyond the grave.

Once I figured this thought out (and hopefully you do too), things started to come together, and I was able to see Jesus for who He is. I live a life in warrior mode in battle as I live out my life on Earth.

The reason this topic is hard is due to the power of it, and the ripple effect it has on families, when the really nasty dark moments in life happen. Some people never fully recover, and those events will now define their lives and affect everyone around them with their negativity from the experience. It's an important thought to look at the possibilities and inspiring ideas that come with the darkness.

The reality is that those dark moments are opportunities to deepen your faith, and you can still shine light on the darkness if you choose. Here is the tougher part. And I still question some of what I see in the world and wonder why. This includes the most evilness of the evil. Whatever you see and experience in this world, there are opportunities in it to change lives and inspire greatness. It may not be in that moment, but depending on the faith of the person involved, evil can be overcome.

We will dig into this topic soon, but evil is behind this. The universal question that remains at the top of the doubters list of nonbelievers is why God is not evil. Even doubters accept that evil exists in this world, whether you believe in God or not. The big question is "If Satan is responsible for evil, and God is greater than Satan, why does God allow evil things to happen when he has the power to stop it?" I know the doubters love to throw that in the church's face. I know, because I was one of those doubters. The church has answers, and so do I. But the part that Satan loves to hear is that no matter how clever those answers are, it still doesn't stop the pain of the people asking the questions.

What I mean is no matter what you can say, you might even have the correct answer to why evil happens to them or a loved one. But even given the right answer doesn't always stop the tears from flowing down someone's face. Do you know what might be the best answer for them? Just being there for them. Give them support, and just be there in the moment, helping them through it with love and compassion, and using the wisdom that faith has provided you with to comfort anyone who needs it.

That will help them in the long run when the pain slowly backs off, and they start to rethink life, and remember the people that were there for them. Those are the answers that they will remember, not the research from self-help books that try to justify evil.

Now I said I would get back to Satan's tricks. Many books are written on this, so I will just give the Jeremiah "cliff notes" version of it.

Once you understand this is a battle for your loyalty, the pieces come together a little. If you are a scholar of movies, you might remember this quote:

**"One of the biggest tricks of the devil is convincing people he doesn't exist!" -"The Usual Suspects"**

Think about that for a minute. Bad things happen, right? It's the most convenient thing to blame God. It's like politics. The one side always blames the other side, and if they are good at it, they succeed and get away with it.

Also, as in politics, if the plan looked bad but ended up becoming a better plan than they thought and great things happen, they may not be able to stop that. But they will make sure the stories related to the success of the plan are hidden from sight to the people, and all you see is the rocky parts.

I remember as a non-believer, I would go to believers with books, magazines and online material that showed the most evil people and the most horrific stories to them, and ask to explain them. Looking back, what was the purpose of it?

To this day, all I saw were the nasty parts. If you look up negative stories every single day, you become negative. Contrast that to reading positive, inspiring stories, and anything evil you come across can be combated.

I can't count how many times I would conveniently get sidetracked reading stories that were negative. Fortunately, I would eventually refocus my thoughts and start to read positive things. It made me to want to be a better person. There are many people who do amazing things in this world, many who have gone through dark moments, only to overcome them through faith alone.

I will give you one example that stood out to me. I watched a movie based on a true story in the early 90's, where a Hollywood couple who plied their trade in the TV business were diagnosed with HIV from a past surgery the wife had. HIV was unknown back then, so they lost most of their friends during the discovery of it, and also passed the HIV to their infant as well.

All three of them dealt with this for a period of time. All the while, they were asking God the tough questions, and doubting His grace. To add to their suffering, he was also diagnosed with cancer on top of the HIV. The movie ends with the wife being the last to survive. Ironically, she had the most doubt at the beginning of their trials, but her faith grew at the end. It would have been perfectly normal for her to cry out, "Why me, God?" but it really inspired me when her faith won out.

That's why the power of prayer is so impactful. People see the true prevailing emotions that come out through pain as you pray, and we find out God is there with us. He knows the suffering. He holds us tight as we battle unthinkable events in our lives.

What a testimony. We can use that pain and harness it for good if we decide to help others with similar struggles. We all need support with something. Use your struggles for good. Share in some form to your friends and family your journey and experiences, and even your doubts. What a great way to minister to others.

### "Light up the darkness"- Bob Marley

Without faith, you can make it, but something will always be missing in your life. Those who are missing faith don't believe they are devoid of anything. Point of fact, faith takes you on a path that shows you things you would have never seen.

Many people believe that God is not necessary to have a great life, and many people do live long lives, and have great success, but as I have found out:

### "They have eyes, but they do not truly see."--Snow White and the Huntsmen"

# Chapter Five

## Double Agent

In the recent James Bond movies, he is part of a secretive security team that goes after the bad guys, and by doing so saves the lives of people who are unaware of the enemy's agenda. Unfortunately, those same bad guys end up influencing some of Bond's colleagues to pretend to be on his side, while collecting valuable to data for the enemy. This plot unfortunately reminds me of a sour topic of people saying they love Jesus, and are trying to serve the world through the teachings of Jesus, but are either consciously or unconsciously showing a false image of Jesus. I will start with the conscious ones.

Jesus warns us of many that will come in his name, because they are false prophets. This happens in many ways:

1. Groups are created that radically oppose Jesus and just bluntly go after and kill followers.
2. Groups are created to oppose views of Jesus politically around the world. They are lobbied against, plotted against, and have secret agendas that are aimed at harming any connection that would benefit Jesus's image.
3. Churches and followers look like they are doing God's work, but are consistently seen as crazy or radical that shows people associated with God are crazy and unstable, and cannot be trusted.

These are all dangerous, and, unfortunately, fairly successful ways the enemy takes advantage of their attempt to discredit God. I may even see them as effective, but I know God has everything in control no matter what happens.

It is human nature to be frustrated by these small victories. They claim victory especially when you know it's preventing people from following Jesus. What it boils down to is many people will follow Jesus when they are ready, not because someone pounds it into them that they won't go to Heaven unless they accept Jesus as their personal savior.

The unconscious group, unfortunately, has equal success, or maybe more success, because they are not being secretive about showing the world who Jesus is. They have climbed to the top of their professions for the sole reason of showing the world who Jesus is. To make matters more confusing, they espouse the exact opposite of Jesus' teachings. All this does is brainwash people into thinking He stands for something they imply isn't really true. People are turned off by this hypocrisy. Jesus has the sharpest words in the Bible for the leaders who say one thing, but do the opposite either in public and/or in their private lives.

You will see these people conveniently placed in the public eye so many will see the false image of what Jesus stands for. With all the ways of being connected in the world now, it has even more influence than ever.

It seems in today's world, even the smallest topic can easily turn into a social war between ideas, and people take their sides, and the media assumes what group will stand and neatly label them into a stereotype.

Unfortunately, there's truth to some of those stereotypes; that's why they stick. Just look how hateful people become when we discuss where we came from. Unfortunately, the media will show the most colorful characters on TV. You will see hurtful words, and even violence on the streets of Christians showing them who's right and what God stands for.

When gay marriage came into the spotlight, the same type of people came out to defend God. You name it, you can make a social war out of it. Abortion. Gay marriage. Science. Christmas vs Starbucks cups. Yes, I know it has come down to if you don't have Christmas symbols plastered on something, you hate Jesus. Really?

It sure does look like there is a lot of resistance toward Jesus. And that's one of the main ideas I want to focus on.

U2 front man, Bono, was being interviewed about his faith in Jesus by a man clearly not a fan of God. Bono's response to his question if he believed Jesus was the son of God was such an amazing answer. I would have to say it imprinted a light bulb moment for me of God's power.

Bono said very calmly he finds it hard to believe that a man over 2,000 years ago who can have such a huge impact and touched millions of lives so powerfully from someone who is portrayed as a crazy person. Someone who inspires like that has to be divine; someone like that is the son of God. Think about that. People all over Earth presently, and throughout history, have had their lives changed forever, and gave Jesus credit for such transformations.

This isn't someone from a story book made up to trick people. These are real transformations. The most doubting atheists have transformed, the most evil of evil have transformed, all with their decision to turn away from their identity and through Jesus transform into someone who stands for the good in this world instead of evil.

Listen, many things are worth defending against the media and society, but how we do it is sometimes more hurtful, and discredits our sincere motivation for what we should stand for.

Jesus says if we love one another, we will be able to be his disciples. If is the key word here. Going to church one day and behaving inappropriately all the other days, and in the privacy of your home toward your family is not advancing the kingdom or yourself. Blowing up social media sites and protesting in inappropriate ways, and being violent is not the way to show non-believers the way of God.

I've never seen someone come to Christ by debating, mocking or even beating people to death to the point of giving up their ideas to show God's truth. When someone asks you a debatable question about God, and you are quick and sarcastic with your tone, how will that help?

That behavior is not helpful to people who probably were curious about God, but the hurtful tones and belittling them because they question God and the Bible is so counterproductive. It certainly was for me.

We all have problems, struggles, addictions, and past histories that are connected to each other more than you think, whether you are Christian or not. We need to motivate and inspire each other through telling each other our problems and struggles.

We relate to each other better when we sincerely share our stories, because you are Christian. A non-Christian comes at you sarcastically or argumentatively, and don't pretend you are a know-it-all.

It's up to you how you respond. Will you show love and compassion to a person who doesn't know Jesus? Will you show them by your kind words, and your reaction to any statement that you can relate to them, and would you like to show them what is the rock that you stand on in moments of doubt and darkness?

Lastly, it's important to remember that when we confront suffering and evilness, society believes that making public policies and laws will fix it.

The world's darkness and levelness of it is beyond our understanding. It is wrong for us to think we can control darkness with our knowledge, and the power we think we have. The world is full of darkness and pain; and evil is powerful and pervasive. If you try to get rid of it, it will show up in another form. We are not meant to defeat it. Leave it to Jesus; he'll defeat it.

**"Being challenged in life is inevitable, being defeated is optional."**
**-Roger Crawford**

# Family

## Chapter Six

### Are you spending your time with the right things?

I think we should move on to another important topic: family life. I'm glad we went over all the challenging and sometimes difficult topics that come up when you are dealing with faith.

I know it's the best thing to just bring up the questions and challenge them, even if it seems we are doubting God's power. He understands us more than we could ever know, He expects us to do that at some point in our life, and He promises to be there to guide us through all the challenges we face every day.

As for my childhood and early adult years, I lacked faith. It spilled over into my married life later. But what I hope to see in terms of spiritual growth, my renewed faith in God will have rubbed off on my children, even after they have left the nest.

I have to say I had a lot of challenges to take on from an early age, both physically and mentally. I'm fully aware that this could be the same start for most other people too, but I still need to share it.

Physically, I was diagnosed with asthma at age five. I had been to the hospital more times than I care to remember. In fact, I missed a lot of school because of it as well, which didn't make it any easier, since I was already struggling in every area.

My parents divorced around that time frame, too, so that had added pressure. I was going to a school that created some fond memories, but at the same time, it was extremely stressful for me. I had to experience dealing with the hospital visits and losing weight.

I was a weak, lazy, scrawny kid. A lot of the kids were bigger, and I knew my place. I had to stay a certain distance from them to avoid being bullied. Sad to say, I really think the only way I survived was being nice to my "bodyguard" friends in case there was any trouble. Consequently, I had no inclination to challenge myself. My only saving grace was being fortunate to have grade school teachers who were friends with my mom. They would take it easy on me by letting me keep redoing my work until I got it right, or sit me next to the smart kids, and have them help me with everything I did.

I thought I had it made until I had my fourth grade teacher who was not my mom's friend; she was not in the mood to help making my life easier.

I started failing immediately, causing me to be concerned that I would never pass the fourth grade. Fortunately, my mom decided to move to the rural area with my soon-to-be stepdad, and put me in a school with a close-knit community. However, I had to take fourth grade again. I was truly bummed, but I had nobody else to blame but me.

I did improve quickly, but I still struggled in reading, and especially math. Even to this day, I can only do what I call "life math," just what I need to run a household and job.

My home life was unique in the sense that my dad lived in the country, and my mom lived in town. Fortunately, I have always been drawn to both settings. I embraced my life with wherever I landed. I think by living in a fractured home, I learned early on to become adaptable, and reacted accordingly to what was expected of me. Looking back, I can see how that characteristic has served me well with developing my leadership qualities.

Another challenge I had to experience was that divorce was an integral part of my life by the time I graduated. All my family members ended up splitting up. A fractured family is definitely a negative thing, but I learned a lot socially from them, which I will talk about later.

With all the turmoil in my family, it was easy to fall into the trap of learning negative characteristics. My path to greatness consisted of living without zero direction, and absolutely no drive to change it.

I was going downhill fast. Little did I know a God in which I denied and cursed was still watching over me, even when I found myself dealing with a delicate issue of teen pregnancy.

What's interesting is what transpired during this stage of my life. Strong, unwavering faith was not part of my life. One foot in, one foot out, you might say. I was going a different direction, but what I was beginning to learn was that God's grace whenever I made mistakes is so humbling. Believe me, I had my share of mistakes.

Let me tell you, the fact that Stephanie kept me around the first year of our relationship is a testimony to her patience, grace, and ability to see potential in someone, even when others saw very little. I was a faithless, spoiled, sarcastic, verbally abusive, self-centered man child. I had no guidance on what to do. I was letting MTV, TV, movies and society tell me what was important to focus on.

I would have my moments, for sure, but they were not often; I was inconsistent. A huge moment was when Katie was born. I will never forget when I saw her for the first time with her eyes wide open and her beaming smile, which is rare for a newborn. That look on her face was telling me that I needed to get my life in order, that she needed a father who would honor her.

To this day, I can't watch any videos during that time of my life, because I remembered how deplorable I was back then.

Even as I write this, it's so hard to come to terms with how I was failing her from the start, though. I distinctly remember my laziness kicking in, and failing to step up as a father that a newborn needs.

I remember playing video games when I got home when both Stephanie and Katie needed my attention. Can you believe it? Video games. That's just pathetic. It's so amazing to me that I wouldn't think twice of playing video games when I got home now if I had a baby and wife waiting for me.

I used to get together with the guys on the weekends, laughing and joking around. Now, a guy weekend is spent with a men's group from church. We just talk and share ideas on how to honor your family with your time. My, how my life has changed. Praise God.

You see the difference on how Jesus inspires? There is nothing wrong with having a good time with buddies once in a while. In fact, it's crucial, but what really motivates us is taking our valuable time and talking excitedly about how Jesus can help change our family life.

I cringe every time I think of this, but even with my precious three children, Katie, Hannah and Austin, the negative qualities I still possessed still created enough tension that we talked about divorce. Rightfully so.

I was barely doing enough at home, and even at work to get by. So many precious moments, so many life-altering events could have been experienced, but my evil qualities prevented me from enjoying my family.

I say quality because many dads are always around the house, but what are they doing? Are they watching TV and the pointless commercials with it? Are they fiddling around the house, and ignoring their wives and children?

Are they sure you are provided for? Are they protecting and feeding you. Are they truly involved in your interests and your personality? Are they finding teachable moments that will improve your capabilities later in life? Are they answering their kid's questions of "Let's do something, Dad," and answering, "Maybe later?"

Take a huge lesson from me and many others with similar painful memories of wasted time. You have to change now, or you may regret your negligence later.

**"Our lives are defined by opportunities, even the ones we miss." - "The Curious Case of Benjamin Button"**

I have forever lost those moments with them, but I would be losing more moments and minutes by dwelling on that. Let's continue to learn from them and move forward.

Yes, I said continue, because no amount of discipline will stop you from losing focus on your faith here and there, and slipping up, and making unnecessary sarcastic remarks in your conversations to your family or friends. It is so easy to get sidetracked with something that really has no added value to your life when you could have spent to time with family or friends.

When you see a moment pop up where your talent, passion or compassion is needed, act on it, even if at that moment it doesn't feel natural for you to do such a thing.

**"Be willing to surrender what you are for what you could become."-unknown**

In 2003, I was close to yet another divorce. I continued to wrestle with the question, "Is God real?" I was at a breaking point, too. I knew I was about to lose everyone, and even myself if I didn't get this figured out.

I had enough. By March 2004 I wanted Jesus to take over my life. My faith journey had officially began, and I was hooked.

My life started changing for the better quickly. We moved to a roomier house, and Austin was born; it was like a fresh start again. I remember wanting to hold him a lot, and I soaked up the memories that I missed with the girls. Things were looking up; it had been a year since I started my faith journey, but just like in marriage, the first year may be the hardest.

I believe once you start believing, Satan tries harder than ever to prevent you from living a life that Jesus wants you to. He doesn't want you to become different. Right away, you have to deal with tough personal issues by using Jesus' teachings to help guide you in the right direction. It was so tough to overcome for me.

The same old science questions reared its ugly head with me once again, and I lost my faith. I stopped going to church, so I just opted out. A lot of my bad habits reappeared gradually, and we were back to divorce talk again.

Before I continue, I want to stress to you to pray hard for God to expose your weaknesses and doubts, and challenge them to work out, so you can become a person of strong faith.

It will backfire on you if you just accept Jesus, but choose to let society have the upper hand and question His teachings. You can't pick and choose. If you do, you will fail miserably.

After a few years of being up and down with my faith, 2008 was the year when I had this renewed spark to start lining up my life with an unwavering faith, despite the roadblocks that kept popping up for me. I remember telling Stephanie that I needed something different in my faith this time, and God provided it when I showed up to church the following week. I wanted to be in the community helping people, which I never pursued the previous years.

During that service I was introduced to a program called Five Star Life. They were looking for coaches to mentor middle schoolers. Having little experience with that age group didn't bother me, though. I knew this renewed energy I had would benefit them, so I signed up not knowing what to expect. I was nervous, but what I discovered is that program altered my direction in ways I never saw coming. But before I talk about Five Star Life, remember this:

**"Taking it easy won't take you anywhere."-unknown**

I remember opportunities to volunteer came up, but I never wanted to interrupt my schedule in an inconvenient way, so I never signed up. And you know what? I never grew in my faith.

For those uninitiated in Five Star Life, it is all about using your faith to help guide these kids. It's true we can't bring up God in a conversation, unless they bring it up, but the Bible is replete with so many values that we teach in Five Star Life. It's such a blessing to be able to offer God's and Jesus's message and not worry about stepping over any political boundaries.

If you want to grow in your faith, Jesus makes it clear you must love one another. That can't be done sitting at home relaxing in front of the TV. It takes interruption of your time, it takes sacrificing convenience of schedules. It takes using your time, and maybe money, or your body's energy to love someone. He never promises an easy life, but He did promise that it will be worth it to live this way.

Grow in your faith, take that step and pursue your compassion in helping others and see what it will bring to your life. Five Star Life helped mold me into the man I have become. I will be forever grateful for having the opportunity to help change and guide children's life. In fact, what that incredible organization did for me was to help me reconnect with my family.

# Chapter Seven

## A Five Star Life? Hey, I want that too.

So, I show up to this middle school, and I'm placed with eight middle school boys who called me "coach." Coach Jeremiah. Has a nice ring to it, doesn't it? There were roughly up to 80 kids during a session, all of them showing up by their choice after school to learn and hang out. In the next few weeks, I started to see and hear all the problems that go on in a middle schooler's life, and I was floored to learn what things they go through.

They were dealing with things that adults experience. It was our job to listen and help them through their situations. I'm talking divorce issues, drugs, sex, drinking, cutting, depression, obesity, etc. It was intense. These kids were reaching out to us for help, and they were craving attention from positive people. That's why we were there.

On day one, the staff told us that no matter what was going on in your personal life, please be there for the kids and stay positive. It was a great constant for them, and for me as well. I knew that no matter what type of day I personally had, I could rely on that time to be around positive people.

It was, and still is, a great program that teaches these kids to embrace these five core values: integrity, courage, respect, responsibility, and sacrifice. When they live by these values, they end up improving their lives and gives them hope and direction. They focus on one positive message each week by leaders who give the message in a powerful inspiring way each week.

As my group would be listening to the message, I found myself enjoying the messages, and unexpectedly being challenged myself, helping me to live the same principles as these kids. In fact, I will be sharing in this chapter many of the things I learned from those four years being involved with Five Star Life.

I started off by trying to get their grades and health in order. Some had weight issues, or lack of strength that was affecting their confidence. It spilled over into their academic performance.

I felt a little under qualified when telling them my advice, but I didn't let that stop me. I knew a little about getting the grades on track, and I knew a lot about fitness, so I kept pushing the idea of going home and doing homework immediately, and at least 20 minutes of exercising after.

After they did those two things, they could do their thing, which was usually playing video games. Video games are a huge issue, especially with middle school boys. There needs to be a balance. Otherwise, what you get is a one-dimensional student who loses traction in his life.

They may not like it, but being consistent with that is something they need. They need the leadership role and consistency that a parent can give. Unfortunately, I heard too many times that most parents don't care what was going on.

We need parents to be strong leaders in their homes. I don't mean being bossy to everyone. What I do mean it's imperative to lead in the most positive way possible, and to lead them for the right reasons, both socially and spiritually. It takes a lot of hard work, but it is so worth it in the end for your children.

I remember a great saying:

**"There is no substitute for hard work; all it takes is all you got." -Thomas Edison**

There is something in that saying, though, that I believe a lot of people miss. When people read the above quote, they invariably say, "Of course I work hard every day at my job."

Well, that is true. That does apply to your job, but the secret is to apply it to all areas of your day until your head hits the pillow for the night.

The hard work is coming home and spending time with family, even after your work day has been exhausting and your body wants to shut down. It means helping with chores if it will help the family out, even if it seems like a small task.

Any type of improvement to your house by performing a chore that needs done, even when you are tired, you need to tough it out and just do it. I think this honors God to really push yourself for the right reasons to honor your family by stepping up to spend time with them. I had to learn that throughout my marriage. I just keep knocking stuff on the list each day, and before I knew it a habit was formed. Plus, I began eating and started taking care of my body better to revive my energy. If you are not used to being that busy and active, I promise you your body will adapt, and it will become easier as you go.

It also means pursuing your ambitious goals, which will require more time and energy, no matter what your work day is like.

It may mean coming home, then driving back out to school events, fulfilling obligations across town that require your presence to make it happen, or it may mean to run all over town looking for a certain school supply needed for a project. Then, if that isn't enough, you have to come back home and make dinner, and read a book to your kids. It goes on and on, and can be quite exhausting.

I'm sure you get the point, I just finished last week working long hours, going home to start moving from one house to another, while dealing with all the things that most families deal with on a weekly basis. It was completely exhausting.

Pushing your body past expectations is such a rewarding experience when the next day you realize what you accomplished. You remember that your mind was trying to have you sit down right away when you get home from work, knowing that most people, including me, would have a hard time not falling asleep, or getting drowsy enough to get in a grumpy mood.

Most days I don't sit down on the couch because I know it will be an obstacle to get stuff done. Now, I'm not saying to never chill out and relax. In fact, that is crucial in maintaining good health, both physically and mentally. You know every day there is something that just has to get done. It can't get done with a remote temporarily attached to your right hand.

If parents of school age kids would do this to the best of their potential, many of the problems the kids experience in our society would become less of a problem.

Unfortunately, a lot of the stories I heard at Five Star Life also included physical, verbal and mental abuse. The more I heard these stories the more my faith grew, because I saw this predictable pattern of evil of a parent who was most likely robbed of positive attention from their parent, or the victim of the negative habits and addictions they have been exposed too. It was always a battle to destroy strong family life, and an attempt to keep strong families from being formed.

This was being passed down each generation. Most of the time they didn't know any better, and unconsciously passed the traits down. Of course, some action was on purpose, and they were choosing their priorities over their own kids. A lot of similarities kept popping up described below:

1. Spiritual Warfare—addictions, drugs, drinking, smoking, obesity, bullying, gambling, porn, and depression, to name a few.
2. Lack of Education--making bad decisions financially, mentally and physically.
3. Lack of Positive role models and spirituality.

I kept thinking about non-believers and how everything was supposed to be random, but I saw evidence of a battle of good and evil going on with these kids just like the Bible talked about. Those seem like great ways to prevent the spread of what Jesus was talking about: spreading love around the world.

What was so unique about being a coach for Five Star Life was the infusion of the different personalities and backgrounds we shared. The central quality that we all possessed, though, was our faith, as we tried to expose the kids to positivity and ways to combat evil.

Our goal was to take on the evil agenda, and change the world by changing negative qualities into positive qualities. Middle school kids are constantly bombarded with an array of negative information from all avenues. We had them for two hours a week, so it was imperative we made an impression on them.

It all seems so distant when you read the Bible, and they talk about all the spiritual battles going on. Then you see first-hand how it affects people and families you know. There is a lot of suffering going on in families now, and a lot can be changed by changing the mindset of how you see life and its challenges.

A huge problem at the schools was bullying. I couldn't believe almost like 98% of them had experienced it. Most of the bullying was because of the lack of the three examples given above, and the side effect of those learned and exposed traits is to take it out on others to feel better inside, or to release anger. The problem is they are just releasing it the wrong way.

One way is to be strong, both externally and internally. Of course, there are many other ways to handle bullies, but I am such a strong believer in this way as the last option if the others fail to resolve the problem. I started teaching the kids there during the options time how to exercise, and take all that aggression and use it, which is a great way to release stress and frustration.

For weeks I would show them different ways to exercise and take care of themselves. It was extremely rewarding to teach them this. I actually had an amazing moment when a kid who was exercising more and kept asking me fitness questions. He mentioned that he couldn't wait to become super strong, and then he told me that he thought it was cool that I could beat up a lot of people if I wanted to because I was strong.

I seized that moment quickly because I saw the look in his eyes, where he thought when he became strong enough, he could beat up people. His eyes were glued to mine as I responded that I would never use my strength to bully others.

I told him I only wanted to use my strength to protect people who were not strong enough to protect themselves. I want to use my strength for positive purposes, and never to use it for bad reasons. He was disappointed at first, but after he reflected on it, he understood what I was saying.

We saw kids' lives change before our eyes. We saw their grades go from failing to A's, B's and C's. In addition, we saw how they renewed their spirits and developed more confidence.

Many had bad relationships between one another, because of school drama, but were now friends because of this family atmosphere and connection with Five Star Life.

We took day field trips with the kids to their camp in the country setting, which many of the city kids were exposed to for the first time. Going on those trips were always the highlight of my year, because we could see how much we could stretch the students' courage. I had great conversations with the kids with the slower paced environment there. I even took my oldest daughter there so she could ride a horse there, something she always wanted to do.

I formed great friendships with the people from Five Star Life. Whenever you coach with them, you are automatically entrenched in their family. They are, and always will be, great friends, and people who have great inspiring qualities.

# Chapter Eight

## "The way you live each moment goes far beyond the moment and far beyond you"- unknown

While I tried to apply the values I learned with Five Star Life, I was also trying to incorporate them in my home. I was really being inspired by seeing a lot of the stuff taught there being useful to my family.

Our church at the time was doing a book study on a book called "The 4:8 Principle" by Tommy Newberry. Before I went through that study, I had never seen a concept where you focus on the good instead of the bad from a unique verse in Scripture. Here is the verse:

*"Finally, brethren, whatever is true, whatever is honorable, whatever is right, whatever is pure, whatever is lovely, whatever is of good repute, if there is any excellence and if anything worthy of praise, dwell on these things."-- Philippians 4:8*

One of the first topics he focused on was how you use your words when you speak. Are you swearing? Are your bringing people down with your tones or sharp words? I have to say, this one bothered me a lot. It has been one of my biggest struggles, even to this day. I have no problem saying I can be very sarcastic, harsh and impatient with my words. Hey, I'm only human, but if you can't expose your vulnerabilities, you're fooling yourself. It was commonplace to have a cuss word or two in my conversation. If I was upset, watch out, it was F-bomb time. When I realized that Stephanie thought it was boorish behavior, it was clear to me I needed to make a change in my life. My kids didn't need to hear such offensive language.

There was a breaking point when Hannah was small, and she dropped a hot dog. I just bought one at a festival, and we were short on money at the time. I told her to be careful and not drop it, but two seconds later she, being a toddler, dropped it on the ground.

She started crying, and I instantly spewed my normal sarcastic, angry tone at her for not listening, and she started crying. Stephanie came running up, and asked what was wrong. Then I lashed out at her.

She looked at me in disgust, and her and our small innocent kids walked away from me for the day. Even with my renewed self-discovery, she was still contemplating divorce a couple months later.

Isn't it interesting we forget many of the good things we do in our lives? Yet, seemingly small inconsequential things like this are so clear. I become tearful and emotional when I remember distinctly how I yelled at her for dropping a three dollar hot dog. Apparently, I must have thought hot dogs were more important than honoring my kids by speaking and spending time with them. I can't tell you how many times I have wished to go back in time and not respond the way I did. I would have just laughed it off, buy 30 hot dogs, and have her throw them in the air.

Unfortunately, I have to live with this painful memory, and many others. It's tormenting even writing this, but I'm pleading with you to please be patient and thoughtful with what you say to people, particularly if it's your family and friends. Cruel, sharp words can cut you like a sharp sword. When the damage is done, you can't take it back.

You would have thought that episode would have completely changed me, but for some reason, my anger never subsided. In fact, it took another year to curtail it. Even if I didn't say it, I was thinking it. I have to say, though, it did feel better having conversations without using offensive language.

You would be so surprised how not using the cruel words in conversations actually calms people down when you speak. Maybe not all of the time, but if someone is upset, and I was speaking to them calmly and positively, their tone would slowly lower, and they seem to be in a better mood after the conversation.

I was very encouraged to see this, so I applied this new thought to all the people I deal with at work. I started working there when I was young, but now I've taken a more conscious leadership role with the company.

I made a personal goal that I still apply today that when I talk with people I deal with to make them feel comfortable when they see me. One of the values we talk about in Five Star Life is integrity. It means, who you are when nobody is looking. Sometimes you have to look outside yourself and realize people watch how you are. You can't be one thing and think and act another.

I make a point to be kind, and ask about life outside of their workplace. I want people to know I understand there is life outside of the jobs we do every day. It is refreshing to hear stories of personal success, and even failures, and not talking about work

I have even prayed with people out loud, even to non-believers. You always worry about how they will respond, but when the spirit speaks to you, it's imperative you have the courage to pray with people. You never know if the words you speak will help them turn the corner. Ironically, those same people who I prayed with remember my years of cussing. So, when they see how much I had changed, they could see they could as well.

Now don't get me wrong, there are times when it's difficult being nice to people; I'm only human. But I always try to remember the following quote to deal with the people I struggle with:

**"Be kind, for everyone you meet is fighting a hard battle you know nothing about."**

What a great way to see that. I have come across countless stories of the people who are dealing with cancer, depression, addictions, death, etc. It really made me realize that these people are going through the same things many struggle with, and they may not be handling it the best way or expressing it to others.
Stephanie and the kids correct me often, and I'm eternally grateful for it.

Something else that has helped me as I get ready to respond to people with this clever saying:

Before you speak, is it T-Truthful
H-Helpful
I-Inspiring
N-Necessary
K-Kind

So if you ever need advice to see if you should say what you are about to say, think about that. Also, remember the previous Philippians 4:8 verse. If it doesn't line up with that, you should just keep quiet on it until next time when the response might be easier to answer.

Believe me, this advice will help your marriage, family, and work. The words you speak are important, but the more important thing is how you say it. If you are being polite, but people can tell you really don't believe or care, your words are useless.

The most important thing, however, is to show strength. By that I mean, you should follow these simple words:

### BE STRONG AND KIND at the same time

This is important. Those words and characteristics are extremely important to me. As I talk about fitness, everything will come full circle. Being strong and athletic puts life in balance.

Now, many people have either one or the other of those characteristics. You see strong athletes and just strong people in general. Unfortunately, some take advantage of that because if you're tough, no one really messes with you. In fact, a lot of bullying and abuse in public, and in private lives are affected by strong people taking advantage of their size.

You then have sweet people who aren't blessed with size, and end up going around helping people with their kindness. You would think they would crumble in fear in bullying situations, but what they possess is an unwavering faith. And when you add the fitness factor to the equation, they are a force to be reckoned with.

Putting these two characteristics together is not normal in this society. You want to get people's attention about Jesus, show how through the teachings of Him you can use your strength for decency instead for what society usually sees it for. A bully wants to push people around, and take advantage of your size instead of protecting.

I know this works. I have seen it firsthand. It's such a rewarding experience to see the impact it has on others. During a snowstorm I drove by a women with a walker in one hand and a snow shovel in the other, I pulled over and asked if I could help. She said that she needed to take her wheelchair-bound daughter to an appt.

I told her I lived down the street and I would return in a few minutes with a snow blower and more shovels. I saw a teachable moment there, so I took Austin back with me, and we had it cleared in no time.

The lady was able to leave with her daughter, and I told Austin that they were not enabled with physical strength, but we were, and as Christian men we were going to honor God by using our strength He provides us to show kindness to others. That example is one of how we as a family will continue to use strength and kindness together, and pray that it will be our legacy for Jesus.

The impact of Five Star Life is not just connecting with students and helping to change their lives. We were surrounded by like-minded, positive people all the time. Point of fact, when you hang around people who want to change society for the better, rather than tearing it down, it rubs off on you. You develop habits, good and bad, which cause you pause. Walk away from those who put up roadblocks to your life.

I know it's tough disassociating from your friends and family, but it can become toxic and awkward. I promise, you will make the right call if you know in your heart you are doing it for the right reasons.

It starts with who and where you hang out. Bars, clubs, and, sadly, churches are havens that will affect your life's goals and ambitions. We all have that internal moral radar that detects when you are in a bad spot, yet we seem to sabotage ourselves by allowing this to happen.

I know I get a little controversial and hypocritical writing this, but it needs to be conveyed. I will admit I still go to bars to meet friends, but I don't drink, not because I feel you shouldn't, but because I just don't like the taste of many of the drinks. The more important reason is I know how alcohol can make you do things you normally wouldn't do when you are sober.

I just want to stress extra caution, because I've been to many where especially the guys are just wanting for some-one to disrespect them and start something. Some bars are worse than others, given the nature of the clientele.

A good rule of thumb is ask yourself, "Do I feel like I need to watch my back all the time when danger is present?" If the answer is yes, I would take off; it's just not worth it.

People do need to be aware of clubs, as well. Dancing and music are great and inspiring, but the type of music and the atmosphere of the dance clubs just calls for problems.

I've been to dance clubs, too, and I see what goes on. Looking back, they are negative. The majority of the people there are looking for two things: to drink in excess and to be sexually aggressive with someone they meet dancing. If I'm wrong, which I could be, that's strictly my observation. I'm not belittling you, or making you think I'm better. I just don't want people to follow a path of bad habits that will affect them in their lives. I've lived it, so I feel I can express this.

I've seen the pattern of men who probably grew up seeing a father and society that objectifies women. Converse-ly, I've seen daughters who watch their fathers act this way and feel in order to get noticed, they have to dress a certain way to get attention. They are asking for trouble. It's a pattern that just keeps revolving around each week, as they try to find love, then get disappointed.

I see this in the world, and just pray that they realize that both the men and women can have so much to offer if they could just see it a different way. All the dreams they have for themselves could happen, but in a more honorable way.

This is for everyone. I know Christians and atheists who do this, and it applies to both.

Now on the church settings. You see plenty of the negative propaganda some churches espouse, particularly on TV and social media. You see pastors in fancy suits asking for donations to "help" others while cashing in.

You see Mega-Churches all over that look like universities more than a place to help people with problems. You see churches get extremely political, and you think they care more about the political issues than what God is saying to do, and you see churches bashing others negatively, especially on the debatable and political topics.

I would say 95% of the image of the church is usually portrayed in that way to people around the world on purpose to create confusion on who people of faith are, and why you should not even bother messing with it.

I've been to some churches with similar characteristics, and I have to say it does create confusion. I thought church was supposed to have a similar message of caring for one another, not be dividers and labelers, and treating it more like a business.

I have a few pieces of advice: If you see people in expensive suits always asking for donations, if you go to churches but hear little on the outreach programs, or say they don't have the resources, beware of those people. They all have the same skin color, or they all have the same political views, and have more stories about politics than stories on helping people.

Diverse people with different skin color, educational background, political, and views on life are what make the church a success. A church is a resource to get renewed and support for all of life's struggles. We all have challenges in our lives, so we need other people to help us through.

You may need help and support from your church that have members that happen to be democrat, republican, gay, straight, black, white, young, old, rich or poor. You never know what someone is going through, or what type of person they are, but you may need help from someone like that.

# Chapter Nine

I'm hoping by talking on this sensitive chapter that you find the strength needed to overcome or get control of these painful and damaging addictions that we face today in a world that loves to feed on darkness.

Being exposed to darkness reveals so much in a person. It's my passion to bring people to the light, because evil can prevent someone to be exposed to love and support we share for each other.

There are too many resources that confirm that addictions will destroy you. It's just a matter of time before they either quickly or slowly destroy what you hold dear in your life. The Bible, self-help books, programs all over the world, and people's first-hand experiences all say the same thing.

I first started getting curious about spiritual warfare and the addictions that came with it from learning about attacks on people's faith and the Five Star Life talks we shared. Another source was someone I follow online, Jefferson Bethke.

The start of it all was a video of his called, "Jesus>Religion," which went viral. He has become a strong, reliable leader for outspoken spirituality through his books and online videos. I watched how he tackled the subject of addictions, which is so crucial in moving forward with Jesus.

The way he talked about Jesus was way different than what I ever had heard. It started to change the way I was seeing the world, and how I saw Jesus.

He was doing videos for a men's program called the 33 series for men. It talks about how men should follow the example of Jesus, the ultimate man. For me, Jesus always modeled the example of being strong and kind at the same time.

I loved taking the course, I learned a lot through it. The series also talked about addictions, especially those that relate to men slightly more than women.

So, if you don't mind me getting controversial again, let's talk about these a little, and hopefully we can figure some stuff out.

The question is, "Will you take this on, and use your struggles in a way to help others overcome it?" This is one of the ways God uses this against evil, to use the bad choices we make, and give us credibility when we talk to others about trying to overcome it.

They believe you, because you went through it. Sounds crazy, right? It's like you had to go through that choice and consequences in order for you to gain strength. So it will strengthen you if you choose to push past it. The "new person" you are after experiencing it will now enable you to help others.

Man, I really don't want to come off as a know-it-all, because I'm far from it. In fact, in all that we talk about here, I will had have experimented, or have seen or tried all of what we have talked about at some point of my life. Sometimes you are lost in the world. It's just sometimes you honestly don't know any better. No excuses here, just my observation on these struggles.

Each of these have damaging consequences, and some result in death if you continue to do them. The idea is that these are carefully placed temptations or habits that basically have one purpose: to destroy you and your purpose that God has for you.

Another important thing to remember is that he doesn't force you to do any of it. When God created us, he gave us free will to make our choices. Inherently, we have the capacity to make those choices that will strengthen our walk with God or will prove to be our downfall.

I believe through God's teachings you will be able to conquer and control the habit or addiction. Of course, you need to put in effort, but most people need to get angry enough with themselves first. Once they hit that point, they have a fighting chance.

I guess we should just start with drinking. As I said before, it would be hypocritical of me to say drinking is a bad thing, but to drink merely to get drunk beyond manageable levels is beyond me.

As usual, before my renewed faith, I always pushed the boundaries on being reckless. I did drink at high school parties, and have actually drove while having drinks not long after.

As I look back on those days, I remember thinking how I really didn't want to drink. The peer pressure to be part of the group was so overwhelming to me. I would have been fine with nobody drinking.

First of all, it's terrible for the body, and has many links to damaging your body, and creating fatal consequences when drinking becomes habit forming.

Another huge one that I didn't think about, before having my own kids and having them in my vehicles, is drinking and driving. Time and time again, we see on TV where someone who drinks in excess gets behind the wheel and either kills himself and his family, or, worse yet, kills someone else in a tragic accident.

Families are torn apart by losing loved ones either by death of a loved one, or someone going to jail and losing their jobs, and their reputation.

Smoking cigarettes/weed is another crazy habit. First of all, I grew up living around family members who smoked, and have witnessed first-hand the ramifications of it all. As someone inflicted with asthma, I have been around so much second hand smoke that I'm afraid to think it actually might have an effect on me later in life.

I guess we will find out. It's a bad habit, period. It's a waste of peoples hard-earned earn money that definitely could be put to better use.

I once heard a fact from someone years ago, that leveled the financial toll smoking cigarettes have on someone. If a person started smoking a pack a day from age 16 to 65, paying $3.00 a pack (yes, I know, it's over $5.00 now), that's $90 a month. Over the course of that time, you've spent $52,920. Now, say you decided not to smoke, and invested that same money into a mutual fund that generated an average of 10% return. Over the course of those 49 years, with compound interested calculated, you would have made 11 million dollars. With cigarettes so much more expensive now, can you imagine the financial windfall you would experience?

The coughing that I heard some of my family members do was insane. I seriously thought they would literally cough up a lung because it was so bad. Now on the weed thing. This might sound a little controversial, but I don't think people should be going to maximum security prisons just for smoking weed.

I think it should be treated just like alcohol, which is a dangerous thing altogether. Yes, I have tried smoking marijuana one time in high school, but only because I succumbed to peer pressure once more. I remember thinking how trying to impress someone ended up being a stupid decision.

Obesity is another one I feel strongly about, but I will be saving this one for the last section of the book on how fitness and faith are connected, and how food plays a part of that. Make no mistake, how we eat, why we eat, and what we eat is a huge part of our happiness in life. Eating is necessary in our lives, obviously, but in excess it can destroy our lives.

Probably the biggest battle, and the most hidden for everyone is sex and all the addictions and struggles that come along with it.

I am concerned about this one the most because I believe it affects more family's lives than any other mentioned struggle. Darkness is definitely winning the hearts of many on this topic, and that's why we need to get real and vulnerable. We can bring light to this subject, and start changing people's blinded perception on sex, and let healing begin. Only then can we watch families start to thrive, once they realize how distorted darkness has made it.

Now God made sex to be a beautiful thing. It's only when people who use it for their own ambitions and pleasure that it has bad consequences.

Keep in mind, these are my own personal views. I'm not introducing statistics or case studies. These are just my thoughts stating how I feel. Right or wrong, agree or disagree, you see a societal numbness and disregard how sex is being twisted, and causing so many problems.

Let's think about each day as we wake up. We leave our homes, and enter the world filled with media overload of sex. Trying to make you think about it, trying to make you look and act a certain way to get it, trying to connect sex and happiness together, is a recipe for disaster.

Why is someone or something trying to connect you thinking sex or sexiness is the answer to all your problems, when, in fact, people who believe this are struggling with these additional problems:

weight gain/loss eating disorders
depression

sexually-transmitted diseases
self-pleasuring/porn
rape/crimes
divorce(affairs)

These are extremely dangerous problems, and I want to talk about the ones mentioned above. I know the list could go on and on, but I wanted to focus on those above. Each one of those helps mold who we are as a society. What's really sad is we have become numb to these evil, misdirected attempts for gratification. It's become the norm, rather than the exception.

Now, look what's happening in the entire world. Look at all the corrupt countries around the world. In many places, women are not treated equal to men. Men have the power, and force women to live each day under fear of death for disobeying. Africa, especially, suffers the indignities or reprisals against women. Add to that the civil wars that go on every day, where we witness women being raped, spreading STD's and torturing them to death.

The men are not honoring God and are doing whatever they want to do to please themselves and their beliefs. Women and girls travel around the world, and are kidnapped everyday being sold as sex slaves, and who knows what else. The men are using their strength for the wrong reasons. They are harming women instead of honoring them and protecting them with their strength.

It's important to note that while there are definitely more men causing this problem, there are good men trying to stop the bad men. You see, there is a battle going on, whether you believe or not, and also that God's true purpose explained in the Bible is to love and honor one another. If all these bad men all over the world would believe in that, and decide when they wake up each morning, saying "I'm going to honor everyone I see today," the world would be a more beautiful place to live in. It's all about choices.

Another problem is the rate of divorce because of affairs. The biggest effect of that is how it tears families apart, all because of a quick need to be pleasured or get more attention that had been missing in their marriage.

This affects non-believers and believers. It is not bias, and in both cases neither one concentrates on the right reasons and distracts by the idea that you should always be looking for opportunities, or if something isn't working at home, just look somewhere else.

The opposite truth, if done right, could fix your voids and give you a great home life…without cheating. If everyone would concentrate on spending the energy they are trying to find other people, or fix the no-sex-at-home problem, and use energy on taking care of kids and spending time with their spouse, many problems could be solved by communicating more. If men and women respected one another more, and find solutions in a positive way, think of all the glorious, wonderful things that could happen in a marriage.

I remember watching a unique video with my Five Star Life students when they were talking about self-image issues, and I learned huge lesson that day.

There is a YouTube video that Dove made called "Dove: Evolution." It showed a normal women with no makeup and a normal body. Then they accelerated the time line, showing the process of using lots of makeup and the people involved to apply it. The computer morphed her face right before our eyes, stretching and applying makeup, and then taking it off. The transformation was both mesmerizing and tragic to watch. The end result was watching a computer image of her not as a real person; she looked more like a computer avatar.

The whole world is being scammed into buying materialistic things based on this image, and trying to impress on girls to look a certain way at all costs. They tell them to lose weight in dangerous ways, developing into bulimia or anorexia. This creates a whole host of issues, most discouragingly into depression. When they fail to look the women they see on TV and computers, they fail themselves. It takes a lot of therapy to release girls from this unnecessary anxiety.

As someone with two daughters, this bothers me. I have made it a point to show them that video and cement that thought in their mind. I want to show them the truth, not the lies, that their beauty is within and God-given. If you really think about it, when you take off the makeup, what anybody ever sees is the real you, not some manufactured person with an empty soul.

I read an amazing book that forever changed how I wanted to raise my daughters. Entitled, "Bringing up Girls," by Dr. James Dobson, he expressed from a spiritual sense how important a father's role is for their children. Up until that point, I never realized it. Your kids need attention from their fathers, reassuring them they are worth fighting for. And the hugs? Hug your kids every single day, because it affirms to them how beautiful they are. Don't do it when the mood hits you. Do it when they least expect it. Do it when you're having a bad day. Do it because you want them to know with every beat of your heart, from every depths of your soul, you will always love them unconditionally. There will be times you don't feel like because they have made incredible mistakes, but those are the exact times you should extend your arms, wrap them around their body and squeeze them until they have a hard time breathing. Then, and only then, will they realize that no matter what happens, you, as a father, will always be there for them.

Now that I think about it, it makes sense. Look at all the problems we are having in society. After reading this book, if men around the world would concentrate on being strong spiritual leaders in the household, it would make such a strong positive impact on the world.

Now, I don't mean bossing around more and being a military boot camp father and being aggressive. I mean to be like what I mentioned earlier in the book. Being strong and kind at the same time will have the biggest impact for your children.

Use your strength to protect them, teach them fitness, and make ambitious goals. Help them achieve the daily habits by showing how strong and vulnerable you could be. You can still be strong men, even when you are on the floor with your daughters playing with her dolls and having tea parties with her make-believe family. It may not seem macho to the outsider, but to your daughter, you are father of the year in her book.

When I mentioned that girls need attention from their fathers, it's important that fathers should recognize that their daughters understand that guys offer a distraction to gain attention as well. I'm not saying anything new here. After all, I was young once. Take Playboy, for example. Yes, I'm going there. Look at all the boys at an early age who are sexually curious, and end up not getting the right positive advice on how to treat women more honorably.

I'm not someone who has an advanced degree in psychology, but I do know human behavior. I was exposed to these types of magazines at a young age and thought it was normal. I've even been to strip clubs before when I was of age. My misguided view on women was warped. Looking back now, I see how powerful the things and people who influence us can be at a young age.

Those women and men in there are all hurting inside emotionally. They have been so affected by their warped views on sex that those businesses that promote it will not disappear anytime soon. But it behooves those people who are seeking gratification to seek their souls and make the right decisions.

I wish I could go back in time and change my way of thinking, but it is what it is. I used to question God why this stuff happens, but I've come to understand that He knows what we can do with our lives. He could easily implant a soul-saving radar and direct us to make right decisions, but when he gave us free will to do whatever we want and suffer the consequences of our questionable decisions, we end up on the wrong end of salvation. But there is hope.

For those reading this who have never seen porn, I know it's influenced by darkness. I see a lot of acting; I see sadness in women's faces, and even painful expressions when they look at the camera. I see desperation from women and willingness to do anything to get attention from men who literally don't have any respect for them. The women are treated dishonorably, extremely rough, and treated like disposable pleasures.

Men see this stuff and believe it's all real. What they actually see are videos that are pre-staged choreography to show men how they should act in their personal lives. Sometimes it makes men spiral out of control in the form of control issues and abuse (spouse, child, sexual) in their marriage or single life.

Yes, men and women are sexual by nature, I'm making a statement here based on personal experience, books, videos, spiritual leader's testimonies, and personal research that confirms to me that that path can be destructive to your marriage.

If we start showing our children honorable ways to look at sex, I think healthy, active sex lives would happen in relationships as they get older and on their own, thus cancelling out the cycle of darkness.

It's important for me to bring up sexual depravity. It's extremely uncomfortable even bringing it up, by I chose not to sweep it under the rug.

But now, I want to move toward the last area of the family section. It's time to bring up something on a lighter note, something that has a huge effect in my life.

## Chapter Ten

## Always be yourself, unless you can be Batman.
## Then always
## be Batman.

Yes, I'm a huge Batman fan, but not of the nonsensical sitcom in the old days where they treat him like a goof. I first saw Tim Burton's "Batman" (1990). That movie showed the more traditional dark side to him.

Then when Christopher Nolan's "Dark Knight" trilogy was made (2005-2012), I was hooked. He showed a very serious and dark side of Batman. The plots were more fleshed out, and they casted great actors. Even the music soundtrack was inspiring. Now, the latest edition with Ben Affleck is offering a different more aggressive take on the Caped Crusader.

I bring Batman up because I love what he stands for.

He has a murky history of pain and decides to use his smarts and strength to fight evil in the world his way. He takes all the pain he has and harnesses it for inspiration and uses his strength for good instead of just sitting around letting the bad guys get away with stuff. He takes on evil the way he feels is right.

This world is not black and white; it has a big gray area of possibilities. If you have an idea or a passion to change the world for good, why not act on it? Some people say going around like Batman does, and beating up people who are doing bad things is doing bad stuff too. There are different levels to take on bad guys; sometimes it's handled in civilized ways, and sometimes it depends on what aggressive steps you take.

**"Don't take my kindness as a sign of weakness."-
Al Capone**

Remember, strong and kind at the same time,
Strength may need to be used in extreme cases, but using
your kindness to solve problems should be the main focus.
That type of aggression is only to be used to protect a direct
threat toward your family where lives are endangered. Under
those intentions it is an honorable way to act if no other form
of detouring it can be accomplished.

There was a great line used in "Dark Knight" where
Alfred said:

**"Some men aren't looking for anything logical like money. They can't be bullied, reasoned with, or negotiated
with. Some men just want to see the world burn."**

I agree with that. That's why I think it's important to
realize that we can't just sit around and just pray and give
thoughts to bad things happening. Yes, praying about it is a
big deal, and praying for solutions is part of it. Sometimes a
Batman-like attitude is needed, though.

Another awesome quote from "Batman Begins" is:

**"Why do we fall? So we can learn to pick ourselves back
up."**

This goes along with people dealing with pain in the
world. The painful experiences we deal with makes us grow
up, and those scars we get from those experiences make us
have stronger characteristics for dealing with life.

The final thought is from same movie, when the character Rachael says:

**"It's not who we are underneath, but what we do that defines us."**

That is so important to remember. How many of us, including me, have wanted to act or believe a certain way, but our mind tells us that we are not really that type of person. We start to believe that because we are thinking negative thoughts about people or ideas in the world, that it's just the way you truly are.

That's simply not true. Discipline your mind and take control of how you actually respond with your actions and words. It is the deciding factor if you truly believe in it or not, not the random thoughts in your mind.

So, that's why Batman has such popularity. People look for and long for others to get tough and start taking care of all the bad guys and their ideology. By using our strength, talents, and ideas, and acting on them could make us emulate Batman.

In 2005, Brad Pitt starred in "The Curious Case of Benjamin Button." I wanted to point out a couple things from the movie. The first is a letter written to his daughter when he was unable to be with her, and help raise her. That scene was powerful to me. I immediately wanted to collect my thoughts on paper to show that my children could always know my love and thoughts for them as they grow into adults through notes, and letters, and now a book.

Here is his letter to his daughter:

*"For what it's worth, it's never too late or too early to be whoever you want to be. There's no time limit. Stop whenever you want. You can change or stay the same. There are no rules to this thing. We can make the best or the worst of it. I*

*hope you make the best of it. And I hope you see things that
startle you. I hope you feel things you never felt before. I
hope you meet people with a different point of view. I hope
you live a life you're proud of. If you find that you're not, I
hope you have the strength to start all over again."*

He mentions another thought that I liked:

*"Our lives are defined by opportunities, even the ones we
missed."*

We definitely have opportunities that shape our lives,
but are we learning from the chances that we should've taken
or noticed? Life is too short and too full of restrictions. Take
chances; it's ok if you fail at it sometimes. Really, it's not
failing, because you can learn from the mistakes, and use it
as motivation to succeed the next time, or a way not to do
things the next time around.

A final thought from this movie was how I started to
view every moments of each day. This is a crucial thought to
those who are wrestling with God, because you need to make
a choice to believe if things are just randomly happening
without rhyme or reason, or is there more going on than we
can see…or both? Remember the first view has no coinci-
dences, because life is randomly happening,

So this is important to remember. All of your moments in life when you run into a friend, or have an event
happen that seems crazy, look at the billions of people in the
world, and all the small random things happening that are
controlling time so precious that seconds become crucial in
deciding events.

Another thing to remember is we alter time depending on how we live our lives, positively or negatively. We are in other people's lives depending on what we do, our habits (good and bad), ambitions, goals, lifestyle, and attitudes. They determine these times of mini moments that cause this type of collision course, as Benjamin Button called it.

Another good scene is when he recounts the horrifying moment his love interest is in an accident. It would have never happened if certain events didn't occur that put her in that fateful place in her life. You should watch the video or a YouTube clip; it's easier to follow. But here it is anyway:

*"Sometimes we're on a collision course, and we just don't know it. Whether it's by accident or by design, there's not a thing we can do about it.*

*A woman in Paris was on her way to go shopping, but she had forgotten her coat, and went back to get it. When she had gotten her coat, the phone had rung, so she stopped to answer it, talking for a couple of minutes.*

*While the woman was on the phone, Daisy was rehearsing for a performance at the Paris Opera House. And while she was rehearsing, the woman, off the phone now, had gone outside to get a taxi.*

*Now, a taxi driver had dropped off a fare earlier and had stopped to get a cup of coffee. And all the while, Daisy was rehearsing. And this cab driver, who dropped off the earlier fare, who'd stopped to get the cup of coffee, had picked up the lady who was going to go shopping, who had missed getting an earlier cab.*

*The taxi had to stop for a man crossing the street, who had left for work five minutes later than he normally did, because he forgot to set off his alarm.*

*While that man, late for work, was crossing the street, Daisy had finished rehearsing, and was taking a shower. And while Daisy was showering, the taxi was waiting outside a boutique for the woman to pick up a package, which hadn't been wrapped yet, because the girl who was supposed to wrap it had broken up with her boyfriend the night before, and forgot.*

*When the package was wrapped, the woman, who was back in the cab, was blocked by a delivery truck; all the while Daisy was getting dressed. The delivery truck pulled away and the taxi was able to move, while Daisy, the last to be dressed, waited for one of her friends, who had broken a shoelace.*

*While the taxi was stopped, waiting for a traffic light, Daisy and her friend came out the back of the theater. And if only one thing had happened differently, if that shoelace hadn't broken, or that delivery truck had moved moments earlier, or that package had been wrapped and ready, because the girl hadn't broken up with her boyfriend, or that man had set his alarm and got up five minutes earlier, or that taxi driver hadn't stopped for a cup of coffee, or that woman had remembered her coat, and got into an earlier cab, the events would have been different.*

*Daisy and her friend would've crossed the street, and the taxi would've driven by; but life being what it is - a series of intersecting lives and incidents, out of anyone's control - that taxi did not go by, and that driver was momentarily distracted, and that taxi hit Daisy, and her leg was crushed."*

That scene is just a microcosm of our everyday lives. Everything we do, see and say has consequences. Most people, including me, rarely think about, "If I do this right now, how will my life be altered if I don't do it?" The mere action of forgetting something as menial as your car keys could change further events. The message of that scene is very clear: cherish every single day of your life, because in the blink of an eye, it could perish.

There are so many movies I want to mention, but I will just offer some that stand out to me, and help me apply to my life.

"Rocky 1-6" and "Creed" (7th) series--the underdog training and fighting the impossible odds is a great story and inspiring every time to see it. I love the series. It's true there are plenty of corny spots, but it's a great insight on his life that I love. The one that gives me pause was in "Rocky 6."

*"The world is not all sunshine and rainbows. It's a mean and nasty place. I don't care how tough you are, because it will beat you to your knees, and keep you there permanently if you let it. It doesn't matter if it's you or me, but nobody is gonna hit harder in life. It's not about how hard you hit, it's about how hard you can get hit and keep moving forward, how much can you take and keep moving forward. That is how winning is done."*

"Regarding Henry" is another great movie. It has great insight in which Harrison Ford depicts a cocky, big time lawyer who really has the wrong view on life, causing turmoil in his family life. He is shot in a freak accident, and literally has to start learning to walk again through rehab. It forces him and the entire family to look at life differently. He thought he had it all figured out, but he soon found new priorities in his new normal. Sometimes cruel incidents spawn a better situation later on in life,

"Cinderella Man" is a great one as well. Russell Crowe plays a boxer who is a good fighter, but something is missing in his fighting style. So, when the Great Depression hits and forces him to literally fight for his kid's survival, his perspective of his situation changes, instead of fighting for ego, money and rankings.

I like this movie, because I know in my 20's, I didn't think about life like that. I thought making money and material things would make a great life. Now in my 30's, I see things differently. I work more passionately on having my family's vision in my head, making me work harder and smarter. If you concentrate on the right, honorable goals for life, you will put in the right work ethic needed to get the job done.

"Legends of the Fall" is another great movie. The three brothers in the movie have very different personalities. All three had both good and bad characteristics that I can relate to.

The youngest brother was wimpy and not knowledgeable. He meant well and asked for advice from people. He looked up to his brothers, and was open to take ideas from others. The oldest brother was not strong, but he was very smart and business like, choosing to live in the city over the country. The middle brother was adventurous, rebelling against society. He lived for the country life, and was a loner.

In life you don't need to pigeonhole yourself with one characteristic. You need to adapt to situations with an open mind that there are other perspectives that can be considered. How many times do we say, "Well, I've always been this way," or "That's the way it's always been." Once you fall prey to that way of thinking, you're sunk. Pride will always be your downfall in the end.

"It's a Wonderful Life" is a classic movie that has a timeless and powerful lesson in which the main character has big plans for his life to travel the world and be someone, but family problems and raising his own family prevents him from ever leaving town.

Years pass and things get a little routine, and he sees the success of his friends and wonders why it's not happening for him. What he doesn't realize, however, while he goes out of his way to sacrifice his dreams for others, he's planted a seed of a teachable quality of taking his eyes off himself and putting them on another person in need.

Something happens that might cause him to go to jail, unless he comes up with a lot of money overnight. So, thinking he's going to jail, he panics, but people find out his dilemma and come to the rescue, and raise enough money and more to cover the shortage. You will never know how much you mean to people, and your consistent sacrifices don't go unnoticed, even though you might think they do. Treasure the opportunity by creating those honorable characteristics that define who you are.

I remember a few years ago the last Harry Potter movie was about to premiere. My family finally decided to take the leap and start with the first one to see what the fuss was all about.

Let me tell you, we were hooked. We binge-watched all the movies every night that week after work and school. Our excitement level increased after each movie. After each one, we could see how Harry Potter grew as a young adult, learning what it was like to live a life of sacrifice. As an added benefit, the fact that we watched those movies together drew us closer as a family.

Make sure you set time with your family, and make sure that no interruptions happen to postpone that time already planned. Now, I'm not saying binge watching is the way to go, but in that particular circumstance, it worked for us as a family. Yes, we like to watch movies, but we do our share of outdoor activities too.

I think I've touched on the movie theme enough. Now, I want to introduce another facet of this family chapter. Music. Although I can't sing or play an instrument, music is such an inspiring and necessary part of my life. I listen to music every day to get uplifted and to change my mood, especially if my day is a stressful one. I can chill for a minute, putting my headphones on, and listen to whatever I feel will get me out of the negative state of emotion I was in.

I love all kinds too. I have almost every genre of music on a different playlist. I grew up listening to different types, and if I like the beat or it has lyrics that lift me up or puts me in a great mood, I probably will listen. I believe many people share my love for music, so I wanted to share a thought of being purposeful in taking music wherever you go, and be able to take a few minutes a day to re-energize, or to reflect on thoughts.

It has been so helpful to me over the years to find ways to quickly get in a better or more productive mood, or way of thinking with the music I listen to. Don't be afraid to listen to types of music you normally wouldn't listen to. In fact, you may be surprised at how it will affect your attitude. The respect for different genres and that type of thinking is what we need more of in society. I've grown to respect top 40 music from the last four decades. I like most country music, and I found myself liking a lot of the inspirational music from different movie soundtracks over the years. In addition, I have a fair amount of instrumental stuff on my playlist.

In high school rap was a popular thing. I really liked the beats. I remember listening to Tupac, and soaking in the powerful beats and lyrics. He introduced lyric writing that talked about dealing with pain and strife, and wanting to remove himself from that lifestyle. Ironically, and tragically, that proved to be his death sentence.

I want to also make a statement about me as a Christian. I do listen to worship music as well. What you have to understand is though you may listen to the types of music I do, it doesn't make me, or anybody else for that matter, less of a Christian.

For example, if I hear Michael Jackson's "Man in the Mirror," it explains what I'm talking about. Yes, Michael Jackson had issues, and this song would not be considered a Christian song, but listen to the lyrics sometime. It talks about looking at yourself in the mirror for once, and saying that if you want to effect change in the world, you first have to look at yourself and effect the change. Admittedly, Michael Jackson wasn't necessarily the Christian messenger at times, but this song was perfect for sending a Christian message through his words.

Because of that song, and other songs like that, I get more inspired by more secular music than Christian music. I hope that doesn't come across as hypocrisy or blasphemy, but if certain types of music help inspire me on a positive level, that's where I am moved.

The more certain churches try to politicalize social media and entertainment media, it actually hurts the faith, because non-believers can see right through all that BS. True faith would love to see all genres of music being played, and bring people together for the greater good, and unite them instead of trying to separate moral songs from immoral songs.

Yes, I totally agree there are songs that are flat out negative and should not be played everywhere, but Christian or not, if the artist is spreading a positive message, and is being sincere about their struggles in life through lyrics they write, it's ok to listen to it. If it helps others to cope with their own struggles, there's nothing wrong with that, particularly if you are Christian.

I went to a service that played a Nine Inch Nails song. The lyrics were about saying isn't there more to life than this? Someone who heard it there decided not to go to a church that played something like that. At the same service though, a non-believer attending thought it was cool that they played it, and looked at the church differently from that point on. So, you tell me, who made the right decision? If music has a positive message, and the language is not offensive, don't look at the presentation and the melody; listen to the words.

It's the same thing with movies. A few years ago, a Five Star Life student asked a leader if he ever saw the movie "Jack Ass 2." His response really made me question myself. He said that he hadn't, and he had no intentions of watching it, because it was movie that would be harmful for him to watch, because he wanted to stay in a positive mindset. I had never thought as a believer that maybe rated R movies weren't the best for me to watch.

As a family we are careful what we watch. No, we are not just watching cartoons and G-rated movies. We are just aware of the content we are about to see. Every family is going to be at different levels of this, but I think it's important to at least talk about it as a family, the type of movies you watch, and why you like them.

It makes you wonder why you like them. Sometimes you have a valid reason to watch, and sometimes you don't. I hope you step up and make some tough choices on not watching, even though it is extremely popular with society.

We have had to put our foot down sometimes, Trust me, it's not the most popular decision in our household, but as parents, we have to look out for what we think is best for our children. Just explain why you feel it's important for your family values not to watch and move on. They will respect it if you are doing the same thing to your type of movies that you are watching as a couple alone. Just be sincere about it, and have integrity with your choice of entertainment as well.

# Chapter Ten

Lyrics of "Lead Me" by Sanctus Real

"I look around and see my wonderful life
Almost perfect from the outside
In picture frames, I see my beautiful wife
Always smiling, but on the inside, oh, I can hear her saying
Lead me with strong hands
Stand up when I can't
Don't leave me hungry for love, chasing dreams
But what about us
Show me you're willing to fight
That I'm still the love of your life
I know we call this our home
But I still feel alone
I see their faces, look in their innocent eyes
They're just children from the outside
I'm working hard, I tell myself, "They'll be fine; they're independent"
But on the inside, oh, I can hear them saying …
Lead me with strong hands
Stand up when I can't
Don't lead me hungry for love
Chasing dreams, what about us?
Show me you're willing to fight
That I'm the love of your life
I know we call this our home
But I still feel alone
So Father give me the strength.
To be everything I am called to be
Oh, Father, show me the way to lead them
Won't you lead me?

To lead them with strong hands
To stand up when they can't
Don't want to leave them hungry for love
Chasing things that I could give up
I'll show them I'm willing to fight
And give them the best of my life
So we can call this our home
Lead me, 'cause I can't do this alone
Father, lead me, 'cause I can't do this alone"

What a beautiful song. Read the lyrics over and over. That's the answer. Sincerely ask for God's direction in your life and live honorably by that direction he leads you in. Things just have a way of aligning themselves for you, so you can lead your life in a purposeful, positive, and impactful way with your spouse, kids, friends, family, your job, and passions in life.

Now this isn't an "I-believe-in-God-so-everything-is-perfect-from-this-point-on" thing. That would be ludicrous to say. God is a perfect father, but he doesn't lead you by giving you everything you want.

My biggest takeaway from all I have discussed thus far is that all the challenges I faced when I was younger could not have been resolved just by myself. First, and the most obvious one, is my faith in God. Without that, I could go no further. And secondly, without the help from others, particularly my family, I could go no further in my spiritual journey.

The reason for the song lyrics at the beginning of the chapter is I believe they are very powerful thoughts on a formula to make a strong and closer family.

I never prayed to God for the first years of our marriage, or prayed for our kids either.

Looking back now, I see a clear pattern of bad choices from me that were pulling my family apart, not together. I thought I could handle things on my own. Listen, you can definitely get things accomplished without praying, and even have a strong family bond, but after seeing my family life before and now after as a believer by praying for guidance and positive direction for them, I see a more meaningful and more direct purpose for our family, and where they are going as adults.

Asking God for guidance and letting Him know you want His leadership is a sign of strength. Even as a non-believer, you have to admit that someone taking time aside and asking the tough questions on how to make your family grow together and seeking positive wisdom is a wise idea.

I do this first thing in the morning before I even start my day. Leave the house on a positive note, and have a plan on how to succeed for yourself and your family by using God's wisdom.

I pray at the table a lot. I pray as if I'm having a personal conversation with God. I want to make positive decisions that will have an impact on how I treat other people.

He is there right at the table as if I'm talking to my best friend, sharing serious talks, laughing, smiling, and maybe even crying. But I still have meaningful conversations that hopefully influence me enough to live my day to the fullest potential.

As a side note to living your life to the fullest, don't you feel so stressed on giving 100 percent effort every day? Who has the energy for that, right? A clue is answering this simple question: How do you build a brick wall? One brick at a time, of course. One brick at a time perfectly laid, and after a while you start to have a brick wall. What I am suggesting is this: Instead of saying you have to end the day giving 100 percent, focus on what you are doing at that particular moment. If it's your home life, give it 100 percent of your effort. If you are trying to accomplish something at work, give it 100 percent effort. If you are a child trying to take a test or doing your homework, give it 100 percent effort. You see, each task takes the same effort, but in the end, accomplishing the goals in front of you will allow you to maximize your day.

It may sound a little boring or robotic trying to be a go-getter all the time, but I simply mean being aware of your limited time each day. I always go to work focused, and try to do meaningful work while I'm there. That helps me, because I come home in the same frame of mind.

You probably know what I mean. You are dead tired from hours of stressful work, and if you're not careful, you come home straight from work still thinking of all the events from the day, and you take it out on your spouse or kids unintentionally.

I found out that if you listen to a meaningful song, or take a small timeout somewhere and pray, meditate, or just take a breather before going home, you will be more calm when you enter the home,

It makes for a more calm and positive evening with family. I would be the first to admit I would sometimes come home in a poor mood, and it would ruin the entire evening with my family. What I discovered was I accomplished so much more by not procrastinating or complaining about house chores. I simply shut the TV off and focused on more important things.

I do love movies, however, but their priority is not to watch when other things need to be done. I will not watch shows unless I can record it on my DVR to avoid commercials, particularly those that show negative messages. If I want to watch news, I just research it online.

Another thing is fitting in your fitness goals, which I will detail in the last section, but this also includes involving your kids in the workouts, especially if they are older.

While you do these workouts or just going out for walks or whatever sports you're into, ask questions. What I used to do was memorize useless information, or what people were doing on Facebook. Really? Don't you think our families are more important than whether someone likes or dislikes a Facebook post? It should be more about what their life passions are.

I also make it a point to hug my family as much as I can, showing and telling them how much I love them.

I'm passionate about people having jobs they are happy with, but I'm also realistic that some people dislike their jobs, even though they get paid well. They stay there for their family, so I think that is noble.

Everyone has passions they want to pursue. The key is to balance family and job. I put all my effort into work, but I am very aware of the time I spend there, because I know I must keep my job to maintain financial responsibility. When I leave from there, I use my personal time very wisely. It's so rewarding after volunteering after work, pursuing my fitness goals and finishing personal projects, I feel like I have accomplished all my daily goals. It's not always, work, work, and more work.

**"If it's important to you, you will find a way; if it's not, you will find an excuse." - Jim Rohn**

Two quotes stand out for me that conveys what it's like to make a habit of setting your daily goals.

**"Live how you want to be remembered."- Christine Re and "invest in your legacy." -Unknown**

The first quote is mainly how your family will see you as they become adults. I talk to people all the time, and many have bad stories to tell of their parents not investing time into them.

They just worked hard at their jobs, and were providers of the basic needs, but the lack of affection I hear from others during their childhood could have been avoided if they took the necessary steps to think outside the box that society has created: work hard, come home tired, watch news and television, sleep, and back to work.

I know I'm being a little general here, but this is a common basic routine that I would like to see disappear. I made a lot of those common mistakes myself, and have lost so much time that I could have used to spend time with my wife, kids and friends and family members.

I know that time goes quick, and in a few years my kids will be adults, and on their own. I definitely would love to hear them tell others they remember lots of moments of love, affection, kindness and patience from both of us.

I know we will mess up sometimes, but keeping those thoughts of how I want to be remembered is important to me. It does keep me more focused on fixing those moments of not focusing on those positive qualities and refocus my time and energy back to creating great memories for them to reflect on.

The second quote is a reflection of the first if you live it out the right way. The standout word in that quote is "invest." It's important to remember because that is the hard part.

The second part of creating your legacy is taking on your addictions and personal struggles on an everyday basis throughout the day, and creating positive habits that correct them so that eventually the slip ups will be rare.

This most likely will be a very private battle you will have between yourself daily. I'm just not talking about the most common like drugs, drinking or sex. I'm also talking about anger issues, being sharp with your words toward people, and concentrating and focusing on what society thinks is important instead of what your family needs from positive affection and attention.

The perfect example to derisive words is something we all have to deal with every four years. You guessed it. Politics. How many times do we catch ourselves talking about all the candidates in heated conversations? Meanwhile, our kids are left on the sidelines trying to get attention from you.

I was as guilty as anyone else. I finally reached a point where I simply didn't care anymore. Having to listen to all that reality show rubbish just stresses you out. Eventually, that negative energy rubs off on your kids.

The gossiping, the hype of someone arguing with the other, and the way it actually splits family and friends apart makes it difficult to maintain a relationship with people. It seems whatever side you are endorsing, you do whatever it takes to state your case to someone who endorses the other side. To what end do you want a relationship to be harmed? It's simply not worth it. I have really come a long way with this one. I used to be exactly like what I described above, but my faith finally showed me that everyone deserves respect.

I have close friends and family members who don't share my thoughts on issues, but I would never let politics stop a relationship with them. Most of what the news talks about is hype anyway. I've learned people want their families to be loved, and want this world to be more peaceful and tolerant with each other. I guess I just see the bigger picture now.

It means I'm probably doing an acceptable job on being respectful. You see, my biggest priority is to be remembered for my willingness to listen to other people's opinions and not infringe upon their right of opinion. That's my legacy.

Finally, the last part I want to talk about is helping others and leading by example. If we concentrate on a lot of those difficult topics in the last couple chapters, such as using our time wisely every day, and taking on personal struggles daily, our lives will start changing for the better. When your life begins to change completely as mine did from when it was almost ruined by espousing negative qualities, to transforming into so many positive lifestyle changes, can you just imagine the possibilities?

Don't' be afraid to give helpful bits of stories on how things changed once you did this or that. You will be surprised how helpful you can be by being helpful to others in the conversations you have throughout the day with people.

Take the lead in your family and show them how to be helpful to the world. If you're doing it right, they will want to, because they believe in how you live your life. If you are serious about your intentions and expectations, while not being hypocritical, the impact you have on other people's lives will be incredible.

Ok, I think I expressed what I need to about media of all kinds. Thus far, I have described how faith has led my life through much turmoil and confusion. In addition, I talked about how important it is to structure your family life by being a good example for your children. Now, I want to focus on fitness. It's the final topic, but what I need to make abundantly clear is how important it is to have a balance all three. Take one out of the equation, and you see a marked imbalance to your life.

I'm being blunt here. You need to have some level of fitness commitment for all this to work. Taking care of yourself and your health will naturally just trickle down into all parts of your life. What I'm about to say next, however, may sound a bit contrary to all I have said before. I know many say that once you start your family, their needs are first priority, with your needs a close second.

Well, in my opinion, that is worded wrong. The formula that took me awhile to figure out is the importance of spending purposeful time for yourself each day focusing on your fitness goals. There are ways to control your stress each day. It's vital to include that in your day. It may seem it will sap your energy to deal for the rest of your day, but what it does is accelerate your energy.

# Fitness

## Chapter Eleven

Alright, are we ready to take on another huge issue in our personal lives? Here is the fitness section. I truly hope you see my passion for this at the end of this book, and I hope you find the connection with it.

**"People always ask why I do it. I'm wondering why they don't."--unknown**

Not only do I think that, but at this stage of my life I want to go up to people I see who I know fitness will literally change their life forever. Hopefully, something might create a light bulb moment where they realize that maybe there is something more to this working out stuff than they thought.

I know I can't talk to everybody, nor should I do that anyway. People live their life by the choices they make, and I know that you can't force sensitive issues on people.

People only make changes when the time is right for them. That's why I wanted to write this book. If I'm talking with someone about fitness, my hope is the information provided in these pages will give them the impetus to look at fitness a different way. It doesn't have to be a chore; it should become a way of life. No excuses.

*Believe that it is undoubtedly God's purpose*
*to impact strength to you, and to make you strong*
*no matter what the situation may look like.*
*God's promises are clear, that the will of the Lord*
*is to strengthen you.*

There are two questions I want to ask you: Do you believe you are supposed to make an effort to be physically strong in your life? If you do believe that, do you believe God has His thumbprint on it? If you don't believe in one or the other, it's time to reassess your life. I'll be honest with you, years ago, I would have answered no to both.

Now, keep in mind, I'm not telling you to work so hard to possess those huge biceps and six-pack abs. Of course, that is a plus to have, but that's not what I'm trying to say. I'm talking about you needing to reach and maintain a certain fitness level at the current moment of your life right now. If you do this correctly, it will put a balance in your life, and you will see so many amazing transformations in all areas of your life that you won't want to stop.

The second question is going to be a tougher sell than the first question. You have to be convinced He has a plan for you. I want to give you my take on all this with my fitness story, and how it transformed my life. It will also give you advice and knowledge I have learned in my life. My solemn prayers for anyone reading this book is to be inspired by what I have written, and apply it to his life.

## Chapter Twelve

**"Today I will do what others won't, so tomorrow I can do what others can't." - Jerry Rice**

I absolutely love this quote. It shows two things here: If you start doing the things necessary to gain your fitness potential today, the promise of a more productive tomorrow will be sure to follow. But you have to stay consistent. No "I'll-do-it-tomorrow" mindset.

It took me a while to realize this in my childhood, so I wanted to share my story with how I discovered fitness as a channel for inner peace.

My dad told us he grew up as an extremely scrawny kid most of his childhood. Well, the negatives of being a scrawny kid in a dog-eat-dog world must have been bad, because my dad was very concerned for my brother and me as we grew on the smaller side.

My dad consistently worked out, and he was seeing results from that. We used to watch the Arnold Schwarzenegger movies, and used to read all the fitness magazines that were scattered around the house. It became a commonplace to have macho conversations in the house.

My dad decided that it was time for us kids to start working out, so by the time we were in middle and high school, we would be tough and confident to handle ourselves if anything were to happen.

He also signed up and enrolled us in karate. As a young kid I wanted no part of that. It was too much work. As a kid, my focus was on TV and video games. Dad would have nothing of that. He was witnessing the benefits of working out, so his goal was to impart his will on us. It was definitely a challenge for him.

The fact was, I knew I could get my butt kicked by most of the kids in school, so I was hesitant to be around most of them. I kept a safe distance from the more aggressive kids, so I wouldn't be picked on. I accomplished this by being nice to everyone. Sure, I had a lot of friends and I was nice to everyone, so I could reap the rewards in case someone wanted to pounce on me; my friends had my back.

I was making some friends knowing they had the strength to defend me if needed. I know now that it's a form of bullying, because I was living my life in a way that was not being myself. I was too scared for that, and changing your life because of how others could treat you is a form of bullying.

But my dad had different plans for me. In order to stand up for myself, I was going to put forth the effort to defend myself. He set up a workout schedule for the two of us to do every day while he was at work. Let me tell you, the last thing I wanted to do was exercises. The problem was my brother would rat me out on the days I didn't want to do anything.

I painfully put myself through the grief of pushing myself with everything he wrote down. I can laugh at it today, but upon further reflection, if my dad had not written down my exercise plan, I would have never done it. To my dad's defense, though, I did notice I was getting stronger. Those pull ups that I struggled with in the first week weren't so hard the following week.

We couldn't afford any fancy exercise equipment, so we constructed our own with a self-made pull up bar hanging from the rafters. What we hadn't expected after awhile was his willingness to let it be our decision to continue. Consequently, I stopped immediately. What a fool I was.

Now the one thing I did have going for me was I was a very fast runner in school. I was a natural, and I loved the attention.

When I left elementary school and onto middle school, however, I was excited to continue my track season as the best sprinter. Little did I know, while I was busy during the summer break playing video games and goofing off, many of my classmates were training for their respective sports.

Spring track started, and I was ready to start winning some races. I still remember that first race clearly. The gun went off, and I fully expected to finish in first. I ran as fast as I could down the track, but through my peripheral vision, my three closest classmates just blew by me like I was standing still. I was devastated.

I was so embarrassed. My reputation as a fast runner was kaput. So, what did I do? I quit. Yeah, that's right, I quit. There was no way I was going to be embarrassed in front of my classmates again. I can remember it just like it was yesterday. That was my legacy back then.

I felt I had let myself down because I didn't work hard enough. I didn't want to be embarrassed again, so I opted out of track, I didn't want to return until I was the fastest again.

I also didn't know I would go home that night and have a serious intervention with myself. While staring out the window in my bedroom thinking of the embarrassment, I had one of those moments of "where-did-that-voice-come-from" thoughts.

As I was staring out the window, a thought popped in my head, telling me, "you are going to start to work out tonight, and it will become a huge part of your life." That was so powerful.

I will never forget that night. Yes, I was full of anger, but it was a good anger. I needed to have that kind of motivation to put an action plan together. My dad showed me all his daily workout plans. I knew as much as I disliked what he wrote down, that was the key to making this action plan work.

I immediately went downstairs and told my mother. Knowing it was 9 PM, I thought I knew the answer she was going to give me, but I had to ask anyway.

My mom and stepdad, Mike, were just talking in their room, and I came storming in. I guess I had an ultra-serious look, because I asked if we could go to the store and buy some weights, so I could start working out that night.

I should have been getting ready for school the next day, but my mother cornered me and asked me if I was serious about the previous night. She hesitated and looked at Mike. He could see how resolute I was and agreed. To my surprise, she thought it was a great idea and said, "Let's hurry before they close."

I was so excited that she was doing it for me. I kept thanking her as we were at the store buying the weights. I stuck to my word. We came home, and I went upstairs and did a quick 20 minute workout and felt so good. As I went to bed that night, I knew this was going to be a life saver.

What I discovered about myself that night was how important it was to plant a thought in your head and acting on it, and be convicted that you should continue with your plan. The following quote is the most appropriate one that seriously conveys what I was going through.

**"The quickest way to fail today is to promise yourself that you'll do it tomorrow."**

# Chapter Thirteen

Now, after that first night of working out I knew it would be a while before I was ready for a return to track.

As all this was happening at school, my dad was preparing to move from Indiana to Arizona to a new job and a fresh start. I'm sure hot sunny days instead of cold Indiana winters had something to do with it, too.

He had a long talk with my brother and me about the possibility of moving out there with him. I'm not sure, but maybe it was the timing of everything going on in my life. I agreed to move out there. Plus, I loved the idea of no winter.

My dad was so excited. He also knew how kids could be, and he asked for a one-year commitment to live out there. He knew we would become nervous or homesick, and want to move back right away when things didn't go our way. We both agreed to it.

My mom didn't take it too well, but if she knew what I was going through, she may have been a little more understanding.

I was ready for a fresh start with school. I was failing some classes, so my dad's style of discipline would help me get my grades under control.

We finished our school year and flew out to Arizona toward the end of the summer to get ready for the next school semester. My dad said he would have all the details worked out for the school when we flew out there.

So, I had my plan of action. I was going to have my fresh start, and I wanted to look stronger as I started in this new school. I had the summer to do it, so I wasted no time.

That summer was the precursor to my method of working out. I was consistent. Every day I went over to my work out area. At the time, I wasn't overly excited about my routine, but I decided to waste no time, because I was ready to move on to playing outside with friends and enjoying the summer.

I did it every single day no matter what. Now, an important fact to remember here is when I say being consistent, I don't mean every day at the same time. I mean to decide on a time that works best for your personal schedule. If you find yourself pigeonholing yourself to a certain time, and the circumstances preclude you from working out, that gives you the excuse why you couldn't work out that day. Wrong. Wrong. Wrong. Working out should be deeply embedded in your DNA. Time should never be the issue; commitment should.

I have worked out 5 a.m. I also have worked out at midnight before. It just depended on what was going on. All I knew was no matter what my agenda was that day, I took the time for exercise.

I finally started seeing some results from my workouts after a few weeks. I still wasn't eating right, though. I had very limited knowledge of all that, but I was doing some things right on a small scale.

When my dad saw me that late summer, he was impressed with my results. To my surprise, the school offered a fitness course of lifting weights and learning about nutrition. I was so excited to start. I worked out hard in that class. On top of that, I did a quick workout for better results.

I made amazing gains that year. I went from benching pressing 135 pounds when I left Indiana to benching pressing 225 pounds my sophomore year. At 180 pounds, I was putting up good numbers. My max was 305 pounds, weighing in at 178. To give you an example, someone weighing 235 should bench 402 pounds by those ratios.

Now, I won't go into the details why I left after staying for my one-year commitment, but my brother and I returned to Indiana for the start of my junior year. I had made a huge transformation with my body, and I had no intention of altering my daily workout schedule.

During my junior year, I finally had my grades under control after a great year in Arizona, receiving A's and B's. I was more focused on grades and gained more discipline. But the tremendous transformation gave me a renewed sense of confidence about myself.

I loved school. I loved being around close friends every day. The biggest thing was I was now strong enough to take on bullies if I had to. The memories I experienced those last couple of years are cherished ones.

One my most favorite memories was attending a pool party at one of my friend's house. I remember changing clothes and coming out of the house and heading to the pool with my shirt off. I was getting looks from people who wondered who this ripped dude was. You have to remember from where I was coming from before I became a workout nut. My self-esteem was low a year before, so when I transformed my body, you can imagine how easily a teenage boy would eat up the attention. Since I've become older, wiser and humble, I could see now how shallow I felt about myself because I paraded myself. But, to be honest with you, it just validated all my hard work.

It wasn't easy working out those countless nights until I was too sore to go anymore. I know I shouldn't have been so happy to see others look at me like that, but that's just how it went down.

Track season was about to start, and I knew that I was ready to return to track. Hearkening back to Arizona, I used to race my dad, who was always a fast runner. In fact, he was so fast, I could never beat him. That is, until one day before my brother and I came back to Indiana I raced him and blew him out of the water. I knew then maybe I had a chance to be the fastest again at track.

My junior year of track was a success. I was a close second to being the fastest. A senior had the edge on me, but I was happy with my results, He showed interest in other races, so I usually won the sprint events, which gave me loads of confidence.

My senior year of track was such a rewarding experience personally, because I was awarded the MVP sprinter at the end of the season. I had regained my title that I had lost years ago. You know, the most rewarding thing wasn't what I thought it would be. I looked back at who I was before I left for Arizona, looked at myself that last year of high school, and I could see how much I had grown. I was so full of myself, thinking I could just win on talent alone. What I discovered those last couple years was if you put in the work, you will reap the rewards. That awesome award was just a byproduct of the effort it took to achieve that lofty award.

When I got involved with the in-school fitness program, it boosted my self-confidence, mentally, socially and physically. It helped improve my grades, and the relationships with my friends improved, because I was in good spirits mentally from the workouts. I was never bullied because of the strength I had. My sports performances improved greatly. If you have kids, I highly recommend finding ways to incorporate fitness into their life; it will totally change them.

# Chapter Fourteen

**"The key to success is doing the hard work after doing the hard work you just did." -Newt Gingrich**

My first year at Coca-Cola was a rough one. I was learning how to drive a semi with a stick shift. I was also learning a new town to deliver. To top it off, I was in a new phase in my life with Stephanie and a soon-to-be born Katie later that year.

I'm really surprised I made it that first year, but being so new to the job, they did notice how fast I was moving the cases around and delivering at a fast pace.

I remember my first few years of my evaluations at the beginning of each year where my numbers would be off the charts. I was always at the top with how much product I could deliver per hour, and how fast I could get the product delivered at each account. They were all impressed, but I already knew a huge reason why I was succeeding.

After high school, I was so use to doing my routine exercises every day at some point during the day. I just kept doing the workouts, because I still like feeling strong. More importantly, I liked how I felt mentally after each workout. Trust me, there were days I didn't want to do any exercising, particularly on the tough days. But I remained consistent and did at least a 20-minute workout to clear my head.

With work, Stephanie, and a baby, it was definitely harder to fit in the workouts, but I didn't want to lose what I had worked so hard for. I happened to notice that the other drivers were not in the same shape as me, but we were all doing the same type of work. So, I knew my advantages were the workouts each day.

Of course, the same type of work was going to happen then too and be just as tiresome. There were many times I would debate with myself whether I should fit in a workout.

I would enter the room totally checked out, but I'd start with a light workout just to get the juices flowing. Before I knew it, I would amp up the workout. Soon, I would get my second wind and finish up strong.

I realized that a huge struggle was not a lack of energy; it was more like a battle in my head. Each time when I came home physically exhausted from a hard day, I would try to tell myself I deserved a day off. I discovered through my own will that I could train my mind to look past my exhaustion. You would think I wouldn't have any energy after a workout, but that is the furthest thing from the truth; I had more energy.

By pushing myself with lifting and cardio exercises, I was able to outperform my co-workers, who would sometimes suffer injuries because of the workload. Dealing with handcarts all day was no longer an issue for me. I even found myself speed walking to get my job done that much faster. All that sacrifice equated to better numbers, receiving great reviews and an increased salary. The result, of course, allowed me to provide a better life for my family.

So, I ask you, are you willing to give up a small portion of your time to change every aspect of your life? To me, it's a no-brainer. I know each job is different, but the effects are the same for everyone.

As you can see with the quote from the beginning of this chapter, it's a life-changer. The question is, can you look past your circumstances and put in the work? Is that enough to make you want to invest in your job and finances? Your workouts are not only improving your confidence and strength, but now you can add your job and finances to the mix. That sounds very personal and sounds very smart to invest in. It's funny, but I never thought of fitness as an investment, but it really is.

# Chapter Fifteen

## "It's more than six-pack abs and biceps."

Over the years, as the kids grew into different stages of their lives, I adjusted my workout routines around family life. Stephanie was always very supportive of me with fitness. I believe she sees how it affects the way I live.

We would take the kids to the park, and I would grab on to bars, doing pull-ups and make a game of it with the kids, or I would go across ladder bars, and let the kids get a workout in by just making a game of it to see who gets across it.

We bought a running stroller, and let the kids take a snack and their toys. The distance we ran was primarily based on their attention span with the things they had. But, as you can see, we made exercise part of our family dynamic.

As you get older, you certainly have to consider making adjustments, based on what you have going on in your life. As the kids get older, sometimes we find ourselves being helicopter parents and engage them in every organization known to mankind; that's what we do as parents, don't we? But, please understand it would be so easy to let the exercise take a back seat and become less of a priority in your life. Don't let it.

I always try to make my workouts so they wouldn't bother other things going on. If my wife has errands to do, and she takes the kids, I don't waste the opportunity to fit in my workout.

Most of my workouts are at home, so it's fairly easy for me to fit it in. I bought a dip station and a bench press. I recommend having the dip station if you can't afford both. Each one is about a hundred dollars, so you can decide which is the most beneficial for you. In addition, a pull up bar is always huge in my workouts.

Sometimes through my years of exercising, I had a gym membership. I could easily go straight from work and knock out a workout before I go home. Those are a little tougher, because I mainly work out alone, unless my brother is available. He has made great progress over the years. He even did the entire P90x program one year and really had great results. Years ago, two of my closest friends at the time wanted to get in better shape, so the four of us made it sort of a competition between us.

It definitely makes the exercises more enjoyable when you are having great conversation and laughing while doing them. That was the year I was probably in the best shape as far as being balanced with my cardio and single digit body fat percentage. That was the only year I did workouts with friends, though.

I learned that I was working out at a more intense pace, because I was trying to help teach workouts to my friends. Their progress and intensity just motivated me that much more.

After that year, however, life happened, and our schedules didn't line up. I found myself by myself once more. But that didn't mean I dropped my intensity. In fact, I just stepped it up a notch. A couple years before my 35th birthday, I had a goal of benching over 300 pounds. I don't know why, but I just really wanted to do it. I weighed in at 175, so I thought it would be cool to hit that mark, seeing how most people needed body weight of over 200 pounds to hit it. It took three months of hard work, but I finally did it. At 178 pounds, I lifted 305 pounds. I was pumped. I was mostly proud of myself for setting the goal and reaching it. I was so focused.

I also noticed during this disciplined time that I was really enjoying church, and was putting the same focus on my faith life as well during this time.

I would've never seen the connection between fitness and faith if it wasn't for being involved in Five Star Life. When I joined, they had option time like dodgeball and basketball, so the kids could expend some of that energy after school. Plus, it allowed the coaches and students to hang out and bond a little more.

As I coached my students each week, I was noticing how a lot of their problems could be addressed by having them work out; it boosted their self-confidence.

Some of the kids were complaining of bullying, self-image problems, and a general lack of confidence in their appearance. As a result, their academics suffered. Getting F's on their progress reports was a commonplace. .

I talked to other coaches about it to see if they were experiencing the same thing. Of course, they were. But, we as coaches don't just throw our hands in the air in frustration and say, "Well, that's the way it is and always will be." Nope, we do the exact opposite. We become coaches to change kid's lives and to help them through these situations. We are always supportive and positive about teaching these kids they matter.

I also noticed when I talked to the other students about working out that they looked confused how it could change their lives. They thought that stuff was for the professional athletes, and not for everyday people.

I talked to the leaders of the program, so we put our ideas together and came up with a basic program to teach them about health, nutrition and basic exercises to do at home. I wanted to make sure everything could be done at home, because most teenagers have no money for gym fees or transportation to get there.

We designed basic games and contests to do, so they would have fun doing them with the other classmates. We also wanted to talk about the types of food they were eating, so we brought in online research stuff to share with them.

One week, I went in front of the entire Five Star Life session at the school, and told them my fitness story of how I lost my track race and started working out, how I became fast again, and how it helped me with school too.

I was so nervous up there, but at the same time I was loving it. A lot of students signed up for the fitness option instead of the usual sport option they had each week. I was so inspired to see these kids sign up and want to change their life around.

I knew I was on to something that was bigger than I was. I felt like I was supposed to be there to show them what I knew from all those years exercising.

Each week a couple coaches and the students would go through simple workouts and play games that made them move around and get cardio in. We measured their results at the beginning and the end of each season by cardio, push-ups, and sit ups, and most of them saw huge gains in strength.

We eventually had all 13 middle schools involved in the program, and the same results were happening at each school. I was so inspired to see these students become stronger and more confident in front of my eyes

I still to this day have students run into me around town all grown up and looking fit. I really was so excited to see students who had never worked out in their life, and when they were doing those exercises for the first time, I had chills.

I started to notice something then. I was making a difference in the world, a big difference, to those kids who could now have the chance to change their lives through fitness.

## Chapter Sixteen

### Putting fitness into church

During that time frame that I was involved in helping the students out, some church members who were going through their own fitness struggles decided to take action and have a weekly class on how to get fit.

They were going to bring in guest speakers and have them give ideas on how they succeeded, so they could learn from it.

My name was brought up because they knew my passion for it. So they contacted me about talking to them about my story. I absolutely agreed, but I thought I was sitting at a table with a few people sharing my ideas.

It turned out when I showed up that night I was surprised to find out that I was going to be speaking up front to 30 people. I'd like to say I adjusted to my circumstances, but I was more nervous than anything I had ever done before in my life.

But as I got closer to getting up there to speak, my nervousness changed to pure excitement. God put me there at the right time—for me and my audience. I was ready to tell my fitness story and share my ideas just like the students I had been coaching. I must admit, I was only prepared to speak to a smattering of people, but with the bigger crowd, I just spoke from the heart with God as my guide.

I played it cool and carried on. When it was time to start, I wanted to show them there was a reason to be excited about what I was going to talk about, because it was going to change their lives; at least that was my prayer. I considered myself a spiritual person, but when it came time to say the prayer, I took the lead, and I was terrified. I had never prayed to a large group of people. I felt oddly calm.

During my prep time, I gathered my notes and perused the Bible for references. What I discovered during my research was an epiphany that led me to write this book. It's the reason why I work out. It's the reason why I wanted to write this book about faith, family and fitness.

I thought since I was speaking at church that I should include some scripture about the connection. I was actually having some difficulty with it, so I wrote some reasons why people were having such a hard time with their bad eating habits and having a hard time to start exercising. I noticed a trend while I put it all together. Both parents were working so much, they were going to fast food places a lot, and not eating well at home.

They were buying cheap, quick food that really had no nutritional value to their bodies. They know, or maybe not know, the ingredients on the box of food are actually harming their bodies. People had trouble making healthy decisions about their food intake because of the convenience.

Then it hit me. It wasn't about finding scripture verses about food; it was about looking up spiritual warfare verses eating junk food and not finding time to exercise. It's on the same scale as the main addiction problems of all the sins that takes control of people's lives like drugs, drinking, sexual addictions, and violence.

Darkness was using junk food as a weapon to handicap people to the point of feeling depressed about themselves. Darkness has a direct influence on people gaining weight until they can barely move throughout the day to get things accomplished. For example, God wants us to serve others, but if you don't have the energy or ability to do that physically, you're doing a disservice to God. More to the point, it makes you depressed inside, because you feel so ugly about yourself.

That type of thinking hinders your ability to help others. That is why darkness is using the food industry so much as a weapon. People succumb to it all the time.

I started to explain all of this as I was speaking to everyone, and I knew I was on to something bigger than me. I was amazed at the response I was getting from everyone.

I explained it was no coincidence that because of high bills and expenses both parents rack up, they both have to work. Consequently, when the hungry cravings come, their fallback is the most convenient avenue to take—fast food. Hunger cravings emotionally direct us to foods we know aren't good for us, yet we eat it time and time again. How many times have you seen people walk out of a fast food place rubbing their stomachs uncomfortably because they ate so much of that toxic food? It not only affects you physically, but it also affects your mind and spirit.

Even if the parents tough it out and make some type of meal at home, the influential commercials and false advertising of "healthy food" has unfortunately made an impact on people. They are going to the store and seeing the labels marked "healthy" or "no sugar added." Or, here's a good one, "high in protein." There's some truth in it. For example, some labels say high in protein, but the other ingredients they put into the product to make it taste better and last longer on the shelves cancels out any nutritional benefit you gain.

My point in this was to tell the class that somehow over the years that life has been conveniently shaped out so people are so busy that they grab the fastest easiest way to eat. If they do happen to resist the temptation of fast food, they are still being conveniently sabotaged. People get so confused on what to buy at the store, so both situations seem rigged for failure. The result is families are growing out of shape, eventually becoming obese or handicapped, even developing type two diabetes.

The emotional and physical pain is bad enough, but the spiritual emptiness you feel can be overwhelming. You are so drained, you have nothing left to give to God's great goodness. You can't fulfill His desires to share your love for God if you look in the mirror and don't like what you see.

I told them that I know that seems harsh and judgmental, and I know people that are still overweight that are doing amazing work for God. But my point was they had such an incredible opportunity to create a healthier lifestyle for their family, if only they took that first step.

Let me be clear, though. I fell trap to the cravings like everybody else. I never gained a great deal of weight, but I gave in and didn't eat as healthy as I should have. Over the years, though, I have gained great insight on what it takes to eat healthy. The transformation in me and my family simply furthers my resolve to spread my word. That's what I told them, and that's what I'm telling you now.

I was trying to have them make the connection that this isn't just trying to get into really good shape so you can flaunt some biceps and abs. It's about using fitness as the center/balance point in their lives, because once you start exercises on a consistently basis, and eating the truly healthy foods on the same level, than something amazing happens. You get your life back.

Fitness truly is one of the most personal/best investments you can make for yourself. When fitness is done right, I told them it will improve their faith, family life, marriage, work life and especially the way they see themselves.

# Chapter Seventeen

## Get angry about fitness

One of the coolest things I saw after talking to the church that night was a Facebook post the church had. The members and friends were posting back and forth telling each other what successes they were having with their fitness goals. They also explained how their faith propelled them to great things in their lives.

I thought it was a great idea to show support and share healthy tips about food and different exercises, so I posted many things and thoughts frequently to keep them motivated.

One particular post I saw was about spiritual warfare, and how there is an enemy trying to persuade them to make the wrong choices. Realizing that God is behind all the positive choices you make with your fitness goals is important to remember, because when you get confused or frustrated about eating right or your workout program, just remember all the positivity that will be the result of your continued dedication and pushing through the hard times.

When interruptions and cravings come up--and they will--remember the harmful effects of giving in and who is behind them.

That is important to remember and maybe the biggest motivation for you to keep pushing forward. Darkness is always trying to get you to stop with the fitness, and just do what you like all the time, which will have negative ramifications.

Think about that for a minute. Let's pretend, for example, that you have a friend who really needs a place to live. He offers to help, taking care of the kids, grocery shopping, basically anything that needed to be done.

You agree, since both of you are busy with work and need some help. While he lives there, you notice that dirty movies and TV shows are always on for the kids to be exposed to. He brings friends over who cuss and say inappropriate things about your daughter while they are there. Then you see your boy watching some of those shows and seeing all the dirty magazines laying around the house.

You notice that most of the food pantry is filled with his junk food, and he is buying fast food for the kids a lot. You then see how the kids are gaining weight, and their attitudes changing for the worse. They start to rely on your friend for more guidance and approval over you. Then, the ultimate happens. You find out that he hit both of them physically one day.

Would you get angry about that? Would you get so enraged that you not only beat the crap out of him and kick him out? You would do everything humanly possible to keep him from returning back into the house ever again.

That's exactly what you need to do with darkness. That friend in that scenario is darkness defining all the negativity in your life.

That is what darkness (Satan) is doing to families all over the world. He is influencing families to get hooked to all the addictions of the world right underneath your nose, and he is doing a pretty good job of it, because the world is filled with darkness.

Let me touch on it for a minute. He talks with the young, because they are the easiest influenced. The media and information the school uses to teach them has been influenced by him in a sneaky way. Slowly, over the years, he has introduced more sexual and more self-centered media, so you start to want to see more extreme versions of it.

You realize that it's ok to do what you want and do things to others to benefit you. As more people get used to that lifestyle, the more people and friends surround you and influence you through the years.

All of the convenient, cheap, and addicting bad food that surrounds you is so enticing. You crave it like a drug, and soon really don't care that it's bad for you, because it makes you feel good after eating it.

You see how darkness is responsible for this? If God is good, and He wants you to make great choices for yourself, and Satan is bad and desires nothing but to destroy you in any form he can influence you to do it, wouldn't that upset you?

Realize that this is a serious battle going on every day, and not some made up story/battle in the Bible. I know you can see this going on, no matter if you believe in God or not.

Even if you don't believe in God now, just notice all the bad decisions that you are making now. If you find any positive choices to change your addictions and fitness problems, you will never have to look back.

# Chapter Eighteen

**An apple a day just may keep the doctor away.**

OK, so we are ready to make some changes, but where do we start? Well, let's start with food. The saying above is actually pretty true. I do believe that healthy foods will prevent many diseases that affect so many today.

Did you know that many of the top killers in people are food related? Diabetes is growing rapidly and type two is growing faster, because it is caused mainly by obesity and people eating unhealthy food.

It is also a preventable disease, because if you start eating healthy and exercise intensely enough, it will usually go away. There are a ton of books out there with doctors espousing advice on this stuff, so I will not go into details. Besides, I'm not a doctor and I don't have any medical information to back up what I have to say. That doesn't mean I can't speak on my observations and research I have done for this book, though.

Another problem is on the heart. The foods we eat are harming our body parts enough that they are clogging up our arteries and causing heart attacks and strokes.

So, with all the medical knowledge being thrown at us daily, telling us this particular food or that popular food will cause some kind of illness, why do we continue to eat it? We're human, so we throw caution to the wind and tell ourselves, "Well, I'm going to die from something, so I might as well enjoy what I'm eating." That is such a defeatist attitude in my mind.

If it's just you who you are responsible for, then it's easy for you to make a decision. But if you have a family, it should be your responsibility to hang around this earth as long as possible for them.

So, my idea is to reverse that way of thinking and discuss the trends and techniques to live a healthier lifestyle.

Did you know that all the food we need is available to eat on this Earth? I have always found that interesting that the nutrients we need are found all over this planet, a planet that was supposed to have been an accident.

The foods available here are unbelievably healthy for us. Scientists all over are continuously finding different plants and animals that offer not only food benefits, but ways to fight diseases that in some case may even reverse or cure diseases that would normally kill you.

Many people who work out are very conscious of how protein intake is key to their development. But there is so much more to that. Over the years, I have learned by trial and error what to eat and what not to eat.

I have learned so much from different media sources. For example, I remember when my wife and I were watching a random Oprah Show, and Dr. Oz was on there. I had no idea who he was, and he was going through a women's fridge throwing out bad food that she thought was good for her. If he would have done it to my refrigerator, I would have gone ballistic. But what he was doing was making a precise point of the junk we have in our refrigerators. One product was white bread. He said it needs to be 100% whole wheat bread. I had grown up eating white bread, but I didn't know any better.

So from that point on, I ate whole wheat bread. It's just funny what you get sometimes from just randomly watching a show, reading a book on fitness topics, or a perusing a magazine article.

Researching online and going to the library are great ways to get a jump start on what and what not to do with exercising and eating healthy.

Even with increased knowledge about what you think is healthy, it's absolutely maddening to read differing views about different foods. One source says eating eggs will kill you, and another source says eating eggs will prolong your life. Who do you believe?

Then, when it comes to exercise, you hear just as many differing views on what exercise benefits you more.

Confusion has played a big part in stopping people from improving their health. They start paying attention to all that stuff, and they get so overwhelmed trying to figure it all out. They go into a store looking at all the labels to find out what's the healthiest choice. Two hours later, they come out of the store even more confused. So, they just give up and go back to what is the most convenient. Fast food here we come.

Well in these next few pages I wanted to share my opinion on what I have learned, and how I try to eat. I would be hypocritical if I would tell you I strictly ate the healthiest food available. Sometimes I will eat junk food, but I am so cognizant to what I put in my body, I always keep it to a limit.

A big helpful formula for me is remembering that for roughly every 100 calories I would have to run a mile to burn it off. Who has the time to run that mile? It makes you second guess yourself before eating junk food.

Well, the first thing we need to do is find out some of the mistakes that we do, and then try to find solutions to them. I remember as a kid we always drank pop or juice. We rarely just drank water. Even while training and working out for years, I never drank much, but I can tell you now that I have seen first-hand that my body responds so much better drinking water. Not what you wanted to hear, was it?

I started to feel less bloated, and I could see my body naturally slimmed. I researched it, and discovered water is a vital part of fitness; it's responsible for most functions of your body, and I believe it affects your mind as well.

When I wake up in the morning, I drink a bottle of water within the first 15 minutes, whether I want to or not. To a person just starting out doing the same thing, you have to remove the complaint that water has no flavor. It's not supposed to. Just drink it knowing the health benefits.

Well, I can understand that. I try to stick to the basics on that, but there are low calorie water flavors you can buy, which is still better than not drinking water at all. Having water containers or bottles on the go when you are on the road will put you in a more favorable position, particularly when you go to someone else's house who offer sugar drinks.

The same goes for food. You need to continuously be aware that when you are traveling for the day that you and the family will get hungry. Bringing your own healthy food will eliminate the need to stop at fast food operations.

So, what happens when you are home? Every day, you have to determine what you want to make for dinner. We all lead busy lives; that much is certain. The easy choice to get fast food and call it a day. The more challenging thing is to plan out a healthy meal.

"But it's so much work to plan," you say. Well, sure it is. Aside from the healthy aspect, I think the biggest benefit is the opportunity to spend quality time with the family. Quite honestly, that's the best part of the day. Isn't funny we can make food preparation as the key to bonding? It works.

As far as meals go, I would stick to lean meats for protein, which helps muscle growth for body. Green vegetables are something I definitely want to have as a side dish as well.

Fruit is good in small amounts too. Of course, you have to be aware of some fruits that have more sugar than others. I would concentrate on those main categories for the three main meals, and for snacks as much as possible too. If you have to eat at a fast food place just try to order a lean protein like beef or chicken and the best side dish available for that place. You will never be able to be 100% strict to a complete balance. So, please just relax. It's not rocket science. You just have to be very cognizant what you put into your body. The whole idea is find the foods that give you energy over the foods that make you want to fall asleep at the dinner table.

Sweets in moderation is considered acceptable. Our bodies crave it, but I have discovered that if you eat any sweets, it's best to do it in the morning, so you can burn the calories off.

The most helpful thing you can do for yourself is researching the foods that have value for your body. I look at food more and more and see them in two categories. When you eat or drink something, is it helping you get closer to your fitness goals or is it harming them?

For instance, when I look at lean meat, I see protein, not the meat. I know that the protein in it is going to be used for muscle repair, which causes those lean muscles we all want.

When I see green vegetables, I see food that is important to body functions and vital for the body to use for digestion. I see milk and Greek yogurt as calcium. I see fruit (dark berry fruits are the best) as vitamins and minerals your body craves.

I'm not presenting things that every other health book is addressing. But this isn't a health book. If it was, I would tell you that you should check with your doctor first (which you should anyway) about offering you some options. This is a book that puts the pieces of the puzzle together. You take out faith, you have no balance with the other two. That goes for all three ideas presented. Food consumption, done the right way, will make the other two ideas make sense.

When you are grocery shopping at the store, there is something I want you to pay attention to. I will use peanut butter as an example here. Peanut butter's biggest asset is it has plenty of protein, but you have to be very careful what kind of peanut butter you choose. Usually right next to the peanut butter is the same thing, but it says "natural" peanut butter. Now it looks the same as the other, but look at the back of the container, and you will see the one you usually buy has quite a few ingredients you can't even pronounce.

Those added ingredients make the shelf life of the product last much longer. The problem is it has inherent side effects that affect the human body.

Now look at the other natural peanut butter, and you will only see a couple extra ingredients, and guess what, you can actually pronounce them.

As I mentioned before, I switched from white bread to whole wheat bread. There are obvious taste differences to the palate, but to be honest, I think your health is more important insuring you get your white bread fix. Rice is natural brown, so brown rice instead of white rice.

Cage free or organic eggs would be better choices also. You will not have enough time to go through each food ingredient you buy, nor will you find the healthiest version of everything you buy, but it's a start.

I'm sure you would agree that grocery shopping is not fun, particularly in our household. Making detailed lists at home and knowing what healthy kinds of foods you are going to try to get before-hand makes those trips easier and faster.

I could just hear the objections now. "Buying healthier, organic food is more expensive." In some cases, yes, but when it comes to your health, what is it worth to you? Do you buy one less box of sugar coated cereal or that package of cookies? It's just a matter of adjusting your food budget.

Think of it this way. The takeaway is when you start eating healthier and you start losing weight, you reduce the chances of getting type two diabetes, which forces you to take costly medication. So, eating the right foods is a way of saving money on avoidable medicines. Just consider it an investment in yourself.

## Chapter Nineteen

### Why "weight?"

So we have our nutrition goals set up. I know a lot of people who make those changes to their diets, and they lose a lot of weight just by making those changes.

It's not about just losing weight, however. People certainly look better, but their bodies don't look fit. You need to include some weight training along with eating healthy.

Now, I understand that some can't do weight training on account of personal injuries or are born with something that prevents such workouts. That's ok. Everyone is different, and they need to meet different goals depending on their fitness expertise and obstacles that they may have.

For example, I have asthma, so my cardio goals are sometimes harder to reach. I simply adjust my cardio each day, depending if my asthma is acting up more than usual. I hurt my back years ago at work, so instead of weight training that week, I took it easier. I lifted lighter weights and did more stretching and cardio that week, so my back could have time to recover, and not do exercises that may have strained it more.

I broke my wrist in high school right before track season, so I did lots of legs exercises and cardio instead of arm workouts, since I had a smaller cast on my arm.

It's all about adjusting to what is going on in your life at the moment. Another example of that was when my kids got ready for soccer season and needed to run as part of their training regime. I didn't do cardio at the gym. Instead, I decided to go running with them. More importantly, I got to spend time with them exercising.

Another incredible exercise is kayaking. I love to do this sport while enjoying the beauty of nature for relaxation. Kayaking can be a great workout at the same time if I decide to push myself and row faster. So if the family is with me, we all could not only have family time together, but we also push ourselves to make a workout of it.

People all over the world have combined fun and fitness together. They run races for fun and cardio training. They go on vacation adventures and go on hiking trails, kayaking, biking, and join sport competitions. If you do that, the bonding and memories of exercising together will last a lifetime.

Even in the harshest of conditions, like snow, people get out into the elements and ski or snowboard. Being creative is important, and some places offer unique terrain and landscapes that can be used for adventures.

Another thing to remember is what stage you are in life. If you are a teenager, you are more flexible and adaptable for extreme sports than a person in their 50's who may struggle to keep up, no matter what shape they are in.

I'm a prime example of that. I once read in "Men's Health" magazine a guy who was going through a midlife crisis. He wanted to get back in shape by lifting heavy weights. The advisor told him that getting back in shape was a great idea, but men over 35 need to think cautiously about lifting heavy like they did when they were younger.

I usually brush those types of articles aside, but I realized that I was actually 36 at the time, and I was actually one of those old guys. I wised up and adjusted with a longer term approach, thinking that heavy lifting would be tough on the joints. More controlled workout routines may be easier to maintain than heavy lifting at that age all the way up to the 80's and 90's, and maybe the 100's?

As far as my workouts go, I want to offer what I do. Keep in mind, whatever I say, you should always consult your physician to see if it is right for you.

An important way that I like to work out to save valuable limited time is to do multi-muscle exercises. It benefits different muscles in your body, and it's much safer, since isolated muscles exercises are less stress to the body and takes up so much more time.

Two of the most important upper body exercises you can do is pull-ups and push-ups. I have done those exercises for years, so I can tell you first-hand how challenging it is to do these various ways to remain interesting.

To make it harder for me I take a backpack and put a small weight in it (25 pounds for me), and then put the backpack on. The extra weight really makes a difference, because it affects many of your muscles in an intense workout.

I also love to include dips for upper body chest and triceps. I like cable flies, triceps pulldowns, bench press and incline press. My back workouts include doing pull downs and rowing machines, along with pull ups for the back.

Not to be outdone, I also do shoulder presses, along with front and side dumbbell raises. I like shrugs and bicep curl and hammer curls. I rely a lot on close grip pull-ups for biceps workouts.

For my legs I rely on natural running, walking, or sports (football, basketball, track) for leg strength, along with leg press, leg extensions and calf raises,

For my abs, I rely on healthy eating. Doing cardio work is so important, because it keeps the weight off. To stir it up a bit, I do bicycle kicks, ab workouts, knee raises, and hold a pull up bar while doing decline sit ups.

These are exercises you see all the time, but the key here is don't wait for the right time to get started, because the right time will never happen; you make it happen. Do your research and see what works best for you where you get the best results.

When you are doing all of those workouts, whether it's at the gym, home or on the road, watch out. If you just go through the motions, and you get done not feeling exhausted, you haven't pushed yourself enough; you will see limited results if you do that every day.

That is why working out is not an easy sell to people. You have to be willing to push yourself outside your comfort zone every time, your consistent effort to pays off.

Just like the nutrition part of this, you are making an investment in yourself, knowing that the hard work you put into your workouts each day is getting you closer and closer to meeting your fitness goals, while taking care of your body for your lifetime.

Your nutrition, or the type of foods you eat and the working out go hand in hand. If you are doing one and not the other, your results will be extremely limited on the capabilities of what you can truly accomplish.

You can prevent so many injuries that you may normally be more prone to get if your body is strong enough to do the activities you normally do.

I remember getting a few injuries in my younger years, and doing something similar. Now I feel more prepared to handle things because of stretching more often. My body is able to move more freely, and also having my muscles in better shape now makes my muscle not have to strain as much to keep up with me.

Staying in shape keeps your weight under control; that's a given. But the added benefit is saving money on all those expensive pills you take every day. Who knew that lifting weights can save you money? You thought that gym membership was expensive each month? I guess the best way to think of it every time you take a pill you know you can do without that you can save so much money.

Exercising even saves money in the clothes shopping department area. When you bounce up and down with your weight, you seem to have to move up and down on sizes. In most closets there are skinny jeans, fat jeans, medium shirts, and large shirts, maybe XL or XXL. You have different sizes for all seasons. That is a lot of money for clothes.

Plus have you ever looked at those fitness magazines? Most of the time the person, especially the men, only have a form fitting pair of jeans and a t-shirt on.

A lot of people cover up or buy layers of clothing to cover up, but if you get your workouts under control, you will feel confident, and you can rock out those simple jeans and t-shirt you have on.

I'm not saying you have to work out so you can look good in clothes. I'm just saying because of the benefits of the workouts and all of your hard work, all those simple clothes you put on will be okay with you because your confidence will be high. Remember, as your confidence grows, so too does your humbleness. Otherwise, you are working out for the wrong reasons.

# Chapter Twenty

## Home Sweet Home

I also want to talk about where to work out. I know I mentioned the gym, and you traveling around and finding adventures, but we never talk about hanging out at home. That's why it's so important, even though you always have the option of still having that gym membership.

Working out at a gym shows complete commitment, but it is also vital to start your fitness goals at home. When I first started working out as a teenager, I was fortunate to have weights at home to start right away. That may have been one of the secrets all along on how I was able to be so consistent over the years. After all:

**"Self-Discipline is doing something you wanted to do long after the mood has left you."**

That being said, that night after I decided to start exercising, if I had not had the weights to lift that night, I easily could have let the moment pass, and the excitement would have passed.

Over the years, after working out at home consistently, and having a gym membership, I succeeded more when I was at home working out. When you are married, and you have small kids running around needing your attention, it can be hard leaving the house and spending time at the gym.

I have countless stories of how I would go down in the basement, and fit in a workout before the day got crazy. Or I would get a workout in before I had to leave for some appointment, or right before dinnertime when there was a half hour to spare.

It definitely is easier to fit in a workout no matter what your schedule looks like. I even did countless workouts in the living room while watching TV shows and movies as well.

Talk about time management. It's also easier to make a healthy snack or meal right before or after your workout in the kitchen. This option takes away the excuse of not being able to find time to do the workouts. It's amazing to see how much time people actually waste during the day, including myself.

That is another secret to all this. Everybody has a busy schedule, and I'm no different. That is why it's so important to work out in a quick intense short amount of time every day. It may not seem like much, but your body will benefit with at least something. What happens is it becomes a habit. How many times have you started a gym membership at the beginning of the year, and you work out like a mad man every day, or at least every other day, and then you miss one or two days in a row? Soon, you find out reasons why you can't go. Eventually, you forget about it altogether. When you work out at home, you can consciously take the time, and then move on with your busy schedule without having to take the time to go to the gym.

As far as the exercises, you should be able to tailor it to your house and your strengths. You can see different options on how to do this by looking ideas up on the internet.

# Epilogue

**Making the connection of Faith, Family, and Fitness.**

**"It'll work itself out."--Jeremiah Clark**

Those are my lasting pearls of wisdom. Short and sweet. I've seen what it's like to plan my work and work my plan. Anything I have discussed in this book are things I have personally experienced. I'm only human, but I also know what it takes to put balance in my life with faith, family and fitness. It's work, that's for sure. But I refuse to fail with any of those three. There's too much at stake.

My faith story is not unique. I've always had questions about God, but like millions of other people, it's not just black and white. What I do know is the only way to live a life of faith, family and fitness is to have God as the center and not on the periphery.

So when the media tries to pigeon hole your religion, whatever that is, into what is right or wrong, just remember to listen to your inner voice. Your faith is a personal relationship with God. It doesn't matter what anybody else thinks. The challenge we all encounter is facing the grey matter in between that you just can't understand.

That's why it's so interesting with the story of Jesus. He never forced anybody to follow Him. All He did was speak the truth, and it was up to people back then, and up to us now, whether we want to follow Him.

Many times we often pray for the wrong things. We pray for all of our daily travails to be answered. It doesn't work that way. Dig deep. Be sincere. Be honest about what you are doing and what you want to change in your life. He wants the sincere talks. He already knows your darkest secrets, and He still wants you. Give yourself to him, and he will show you how to live in a world that many struggle with.

You will still have the same problems to deal with as others who don't believe, but you will not be the same person as far as how you deal with those problems again.

People fall short of their potential every day, including myself, but when I make mistakes, I pray to God for forgiveness, and then I can approach the day without that burdensome weight on shoulders.

That is the thing to be aware of. When you see a believer you know, and they screw up, watch how they realize what they have done and how they fix it. That shows sincerity.

If you do decide to start looking to God for answers, don't give up, because you see things happen in the world you don't have answers for. When you are sincere with God, everything will "work itself out."

Looking back at my life without a convicted faith, I can see how my life has changed for the better with an unwavering faith. Of course, I scratch my head sometimes, saying, "I don't get it, God," or "Why is this happening to me, God?"

But I am assured by the awesome grace of God that I can survive with a new attitude. At times, I think I don't deserve grace, but God looks at your heart and knows who you are.

God has shown me how people can change not only themselves but totally change their whole family legacy by how they live. They make sure their loved ones are growing emotionally in a way that makes this world a better place to live in. That is such a cool thing.

**"Be the Change you want to see in the world!"**

If you truly want to see change, we all need to make the changes. Of course, you can make positive changes in the world without God, but I have experienced that to truly be the most impactful, you need to have something bigger on your side.

Seeing my kids being kind to others and treating them with respect and honor is an agent of change I am so proud of. In my previous life of faithlessness, I could have easily taught them to not watch out for others and screw everyone else. Those types of people are just lost.

It doesn't make them bad people; they just need the kindness, strength and compassion that God can provide. Some day they might see that. That is where the hope comes in for the world. For me, that is my sense of purpose. I want to elicit change, so that other people can make the world better.

When my faith was strong, my family life was strong, and when I found my fitness goals starting to not only make me strong physically, the discipline it taught me slowly started to help me take on the same problems and choices I needed to make in my faith and family life.

Discipline. Focus. Consistency. Intensity. Perseverance. These are all traits that fitness teaches you. What I didn't know at the time was those same traits taught me everything that would help my family survive in the world.

Those traits are all traits of God, and not darkness. Darkness will influence you to be the opposite of that. That is how you know if you are going the right direction in your life. If you are not living with those traits above to maintain your goals, then I would highly recommend praying to God for another path. Together you can change into the person you were meant to be.

Becoming strong from the workouts in fitness is awesome, and it gives you so many more possibilities in life, but the best part about it is how that strength can be used for so much more. When you apply those traits needed to maintain that strength, your family will be able to follow a path that God wants you to follow and to live a life honorably.

# My Humble Prayer

Father, it has been a huge struggle for me to finish this book. Distractions and struggles came from every direction.

I know only through your love and strength, I was able to finish this book. I have had many mixed emotions, but I was motived to inspire people. I smiled at the memories that brought me joy. I frowned when I had to expose my vulnerable past. Writing this book was unexpectedly therapeutic and helped me to know that your grace is awesome. You wanted me to write this book.

Father, I pray for others who are struggling now. It's a tough world, and I want others to see as I did that we need the kindness and strength that only you can give.

I have tried it without you, and I failed miserably. For anyone out there in need, please take anything from this book and use it in the way it needs to be used.

What an honor it would be for me if you used it.

Father, I pray every day for people just to be curious about your power, and what you are capable of. I know you will lead them to paths in their lives that they didn't know existed if they let you into their lives. I ask this through the powerful name of Jesus, Amen.

## Be Strong and Be Kind

These books helped guide me in the right direction over the years, and I highly recommend them:

"Jesus>Religion" - Jefferson Bethke
"It's Not What You Think"- Jefferson Bethke
"The 4:8 Principle"- Tommy Newberry
"Bringing Up Girls"- Dr. James Dobson
"Bringing Up Boys"- Dr. James Dobson
"Radical"- David Platt
"Counterfeit Gods"- Timothy Keller
"Crazy Love" - Francis Chan
"The Last Lecture"- Randy Pausch
"Fight" -Craig Groeschel
"Not a Fan"- Kyle Idleman
"Daniel Plan"- Rick Warren
"Wild at Heart"- John Eldridge
"Gospel"- JD Greear
"Bring It" - Tony Horton
"Through the Eyes of a Lion"- Levi Lusko
"One Thousand Gifts"- Ann Voskamp
"Prodigal God"- Timothy Keller
"Beautiful Outlaw"- John Eldridge
"Ragamuffin Gospel"- Bremmen Manning
"Follow Me" - David Platt
"Fireproof" - Alex and Stephen Kendrick

Here are some movies below I used in this book, and are accredited to helping me become more inspired about life.

"It's a Wonderful Life"
"Legends of the Fall"
"Cinderella Man"
"Harry Potter Collection"
"Regarding Henry"
The Dark Knight Trilogy
"The Curious Case of Benjamin Button"
"Rocky 1-6" and "Creed"

Three standout magazines that help me with fitness, and should be acknowledged

"Men's Health"
"Men's Fitness"
"Muscle and Fitness"